The Moment You're In

Rose Gold Publishing, LLC

The Moment You're In

How I Found My Presence in the Present

Kaitlynn Mika

Acknowledgements

My Coaches:

- ### MARK ENGLAND:

Mark England is the co-founder and head coach of Enlifted. He has been researching, presenting, and coaching on the power of words and stories for the past 16 years. He has a Master's Degree in Education and was an elementary school physical education teacher before transitioning into personal development.

enlifted.me

- ### MATT GARDINER

Recovery Coach || Storywork Coach || Sound Therapist

"It's not the circumstance that gets you, it's your STORY about the circumstance that gets you."

Matt Gardiner is a Recovery Coach & Storywork Coach who has helped numerous people get out of their 'stuck stories' and manage their addictions to effectively integrate sobriety into their lives. His coaching method focuses on breath awareness, inner dialogue word choice, and reframing the stories you've been attaching to the events of your life.

"Change Your Story, Change Your Life".

Matt's 3-Step Program explores: *Sober Socializing, Habits & Routines and Emotional Management.* Matt is also a lifelong musician and Sound Therapist, which complements his work as a Coach.

'Beyond Recovery' is a podcast hosted by Matt, where guests come on to share their journeys of recovery.

@recoveryroadmap.me (IG)
www.recoveryroadmap.me
https://linktr.ee/mattgardiner555

@mattgardinerLIVE (Facebook & YouTube)
Beyond Recovery (podcast)

- KIMBERLY KESTING

Kimberly Kesting is a health & mindset coach. She is the host of the Get Enlifted podcast and the Head of Growth for Enlifted, a mindset coaching program for coaches and leaders. In her free time, you'll find her writing or creating art, out in nature, shopping the local farmers markets, or her favorite hobby, cheffing it up in the kitchen and sharing the magic of food.
enlifted.me

Featured Artists

Cover Illustration created by Martha Freewalt, the owner of Sageside Collective and a dear friend of the author. Soundtrack created by Matt Gardiner. https://mattwgardiner.bandcamp.com/album/the-moment-youre-in-soundtrack.

Dedication

"Dedicated to you, the reader. This book is left intentionally imperfect to remind you that even with flaws, we are still art."

-Kaitlynn Mika

The Moment You're In

How I Found My Presence in the Present

Kaitlynn Mika

Table of Contents

Acknowledgments   iv
Dedication   vi
From Victim to Hero   ix

Chapter 1: My Story   7
Chapter 2: Realization   37
Chapter 3: Patterns   57
Chapter 4: Unlearn   67
Chapter 5: Nourish   81
Chapter 6: Breathe   93
Chapter 7: Move   101
Chapter 8: Words   112
Chapter 9: Recreate   129
Chapter 10: Redefine   146
Chapter 11: Allow   162
Chapter 12: Expand   170
Chapter 13: Set You Free   180

You are Now and Now is Love   187

About the Author   194

From Victim to Hero

I stood in the kitchen.
I yelled, I cried,
lost all control,
feeling nothing inside

Off the counter
I picked up a knife,
I threatened right there,
to end my life.

The police were called,
I went without a fight,
In a hospital
I spent the night.

I woke up the next day,
feeling confused,
feeling broken,
my body abused.

I was losing myself,
letting go of my grip,
down and down-
how did I slip?

I knew I had to change.
I had to start the shift,
up out of that hole,
myself, I had to lift.

I started to change.
I began to heal.
I stopped running from myself,
and started to feel.

I started looking at myself
again in the mirror.
Through tears, I had me
and held myself near.

I asked for help
and accepted it all.
It was my time to get up-
the end of my fall.

I look back on that night,
glad it went down
because it was the change I needed
when I turned my life around.

And look at me now,
standing so free!
Look at me here,
I returned to me.

Welcome to my life. I will start by telling you about my story of living life as a victim to turning myself into my hero. First, let me define the victim mentality.

"The victim mentality is an acquired personality trait in which a person tends to regard themselves as the victim of the negative actions of others, even in the absence of clear evidence. The victim mentality depends on a habitual thought process." And man, was my thought process habitual? I believed that life was happening to me, and I was rolling with the punches, more like getting pummeled by them.

Even as a kid, before I can remember, I had a fear of confrontation, a fear of getting in trouble. To the point that there were multiple occasions in which I would get so upset that I would cry until I passed out.

In grade school, whenever a teacher would correct my behavior (even in a kind way), I would get embarrassed and cry. Even as I type this, I wonder where it came from and why I was so afraid to be in trouble. Is this why I made myself the victim? Was it easier that way than accepting responsibility for all of life, the good and the bad?

In high school, I was timid. I wouldn't talk to many people and only had a few friends. I would spend my lunch breaks in classrooms with teachers doing homework instead of with my peers. I had a fear of my voice, and that people would not care or think what I had to say was dumb. These were the things I said to myself. I didn't try out for the high school softball team, a sport I had grown to love, because I was scared. What if the girls were mean? What if they didn't like me? A projection, as nobody could be meaner to me than I was to me or dislike me as much as I despised myself. And all made up in my head.

I would tell myself I wasn't good enough to do this or strong enough to do that. I wasn't pretty enough for anyone to like me.

No matter what was happening then, I trained my brain to look for the negative aspect of any experience.

During my senior year, I started working in a restaurant and made friends who drank and could get alcohol. I started drinking, and that voice would quiet, and I felt like I could talk to people and relax. I felt like I could be myself. I went to college with that same belief, and then those "bad things" I had been training myself to see would happen to me. I would drink, and I could stop the feeling and the voices that worked against me.

Soon, unknowingly, I drank if any emotion was uncomfortable for me to feel. During celebrations – I drank. During grief, I drank. When I was overwhelmed, I drank.

And at the same time, I was emotionally eating or yo-yo dieting to focus on something besides what I was feeling. I would continue this cycle of feeling bad about myself, feeling bad for myself. I did things to make myself feel worse, thinking they made it better.

It took a few more years for me to realize it, though. I got out of college, and I had no self-awareness. I lived on autopilot for the next eight years. Wake-up call after wake-up call, telling me something needed to change. These wake-up calls were trying to shift my path, and I had no idea how to listen to them or that they were even there.

I met my now-husband, and I started carrying myself on his love, happiness, and ability to be in the moment. And sure, that worked for a while, and then after the initial honeymoon period, it started to dwindle. I found myself back in the darkness. We got engaged in December 2019 and picked September 19th, 2020, as our wedding date. I was already unsteady, and now I entered the uncertainty of wedding planning during the COVID-19 pandemic.

I was drinking more. I was unaware of my eating habits, as I was spending all my time and energy planning my wedding while working full-time. I gave myself every excuse, "I am stressed. Look what I am going through; what did I do to deserve this?" Those were some things I said to myself as I ordered takeout and opened a bottle of wine at 3:30 pm on a Tuesday.

After we postponed our big party and decided to get married in a small ceremony in my parent's backyard, I continued to be my victim. I gave myself all the excuses to continue fighting instead of loving and helping myself. Then the big wake-up call happened.

I was on a girls' weekend, and it was booze-filled, and I was utterly disconnected from anything close to my authentic self. I only focused on my next drink. When we got home from the bar (already blacked out), I decided that I wanted to keep drinking and got lost trying to get to the lobby bar. After returning to my hotel room, I argued with the others there. (Mind you, I have no memory of this). At some point, I threatened to hurt myself, and they called the police. I landed in the hospital until the next day.

That was the big wake-up call I needed. What I thought at the time was the worst thing I ever went through was the shift. I knew I had given myself away at that point, and I had let any light that used to be inside me go out. I thought I was at rock bottom. I look back now; the person writing this story does not exist without going through what I did. So even though I was "at the end of my rope" in my mind, I slowly started climbing up.

I entered coaching, started looking into myself, and started healing myself. I went into my stories from the past. Overeating, Shit-talking myself, and being dependent on drinking were symptoms of the real problem, coping mechanisms for my real problem. Even though I had become dependent on these things, none of these were my addiction.

I was addicted to my victim mentality.

Without the awareness of myself and after living the way I was for so long; I didn't even realize it until I started doing the work on myself. I learned that all the stories I told myself could be changed. I could stop looking at them as the reason I was broken and start using them as my power.

I realized that when it came down to it, all I had to do was look for the good, see the good, and see the beauty. And there is so much beauty. So, I started living that way instead. I began to focus on what I was, what I could do, and who I wanted to be. I learned that the source of all love is self-love. I learned to relight my light.

The person I am now could not exist without all that has happened in my past. I am so proud of those past versions of me. I am here now because of everything that has happened in my life. I get to choose how I react to everything in my life. I became my hero because of everything that has happened in my life.

And I am grateful for it all.

This is the story of my journey and what a journey it has been. These are my words and my experiences. I have learned of so many gifts in this life and that they were within me all along. I need to share those with the world, which is why this book is so important. Thank you for reading this book and taking this adventure with me. Remember that you hold all of your power, and you are already worthy of all that you are, all that you desire, and all that you will be.

Your story may look different than mine, and if you reach for this book, you are ready to live in the moment. My moments are mine, and yours will be yours. What we have in common is that we both get to have journeys, and we are both on the path to feeling it all and seeing it all. If you want to live in each moment fully, you are in the right place. I will tell you how I got here, Now, and I will give you the keys to the car that I used to drive myself here.

Much love to you, enjoy and remember you are infinitely powerful already.

Chapter 1:
My Story

What did I do
To make my life mine?
How did I finally
let myself shine?

When did I learn
the moment I'm in?
When did I decide
To win?

What I'll say is this;
it is hard to say,
if it was one big moment,
Or day by day.

I had wake-up calls,
some big, some small
and surely, I didn't
catch them all.

I started sweet,
and stayed that way,
And my wanting to stay sweet,
started eating me away.
I couldn't express myself,

I couldn't be free.
I couldn't shine bright,
I couldn't be me.

Until I learned,
everything is inside,
and the beauty in me,
was what I would hide.

So, I stopped hiding,
and I let myself grow.
Inside me,
I began to know.

Little Kaitlynn was a shy, sweet, and timid girl, afraid of her shadow and glued to her parents. Still, she was full of love. All she wanted to do was make people smile, make people happy, and be good for everyone else.

I remember the many times when people would say, "you are just so sweet" or "you think about everyone else before yourself." I was a little girl with a huge heart, sometimes too big for my good.

At a glance, my childhood was typical and beautiful. I grew up well, and for the most part, that is true. I had all the external things that make a childhood good. I had attentive parents, a roof over my head, food, water, shelter, and love. I grew up in a friendly neighborhood. I was so blessed by all of those things. I can see that now, and it is beautiful.

At the time, I pressured myself to be good, to make sure *I didn't cause upset.* I had high expectations of myself and learned to disappoint myself repeatedly. I became my worst enemy.

Where did it all start? How did I get to a place where I considered myself a victim? What happened in my childhood, or earlier, to get me to a place where I didn't want to take responsibility for anything? When did I start to put so much pressure on myself to be good, leading me to believe I was never good enough?

Throughout childhood, I was labeled as over-sensitive, over-emotional, fragile, and made of glass. You name it. Only recently did I learn about the personality trait of being a highly sensitive person (HSP).

I was the sweet one, the one that cried about everything. It was considered innate, a part of my nature. I felt a lot and couldn't control my emotions.

I don't know when this started but knowing that I am an HSP explains why I can't remember when I began to feel so over-emotional. Now, reflecting on some of my earliest moments of feeling everything so intensely is so interesting.

The first time something happened, I got so upset that I cried until I passed out. I was two, climbing up the stairs, and I was not supposed to be on the stairs. I hit my head and was crying, so my mom came over and said to me and said: "Kaitlynn, why were you playing on the stairs?" I started crying harder, even more, upset because I thought I was in trouble, and I cried so hard that I ended up passing out from lack of oxygen. My mom ran to our neighbor's house with me in her arms, and I came to about twenty seconds later.

A couple of years later, my older brother and I fought on the way home from the bus stop. This was a fight we had for days. The argument was whether we were watching Ninja Turtles or Wizard of Oz when we got home. With me exhausted from the battle, my mom exclaimed, "I have had it with this argument," and walked ahead. The next thing she hears is my brother say, "Uh, mom," and she turned around, and there I was, passed out in the street.

These are funny stories to me now, and I still look back and wonder why? Why was I so scared of disappointing people? Why was I so frightened of angering people? Why did I want to be good and approved of so desperately?

The last story from "before I can remember" childhood that I will tell is a story that happened in first grade. I had used a stamp on my desk at school, and the teacher came over and said, "Kaitlynn, we don't stamp on our desks."

And that *Leveled* me.

I cried and cried and cried until my mom had to come and pick me up.

I remember priding myself and basing my worth on people telling me I was so sweet and kind. I was well-behaved; that was my identity. I wanted people's compliments; I wanted people's affirmation. I spent a lot of energy trying to be good enough for others. It rarely mattered to me what I thought.

I loved to sing, and I was untrained, and my voice was undeveloped. My singing was dismissed as something cute. It made people smile when I was young, so I based a happy sentiment on singing. I was doing what my heart loved when I sang. As I grew into an older child, people's words changed. Eye rolls, laughter, or being told I was annoying. I was also often told I was tone-deaf and couldn't sing. I grew to believe that my singing was annoying. And by basing my life on making others happy, my happiness became unimportant and irrelevant. Even though I clung to it for as long as possible, I gave up. It was unrealistic to think I could sing, and no way I could be a singer. It is way too hard to "make it" in that industry…I was tone-deaf anyway, so what was the use of trying?

I told myself, "I could write songs. I would be a songwriter. That's hard to get into, too, though, and you still have to be able to carry a tune to do that. Maybe I'll write greeting cards. I like to write people cards on their birthdays."

I started compromising what I loved because if others didn't approve of it, why would it matter? If I couldn't love myself, how could I love anything?

Running on other people's approval became the only thing I "wanted". I wanted people to love me, or I wanted to be invisible to them. Those traits were also reinforced. Sitting quietly and speaking when spoken to earned me the title of a good kid, a polite kid, and as mentioned above, that was all that I strived for. So, I was sitting quietly, getting told I was so sweet, and I continued to sit quietly until it was a pattern.

People were right when they called me sweet, an innate trait. That still is an inherent trait. Now, as an adult, I want to show people how to be happy. The difference is the little me was so focused on making other people happy that I forgot about my happiness... I was so concerned with making other people smile that I lost mine. Little Kaitlynn was infinite love, a gem, a light in this world.

Those things were my gifts when I was young, and as I grew, "human logic" took over, and I put out that light. That little girl deserved to shine, not be darkened.

Most of the things that little Kaitlynn loved turned into silly dreams. They didn't matter. What mattered was ensuring she was liked by the people around her or, at least, that they did not dislike her.

As a young girl, I was obsessed with the fear of not being liked by others.

No Longer a Kid

At thirteen, I developed a toxic relationship with my body image. The way that I looked at myself is so sad to me now. I was a healthy and beautiful girl. I entered my teenage years and put myself down daily. I would tell myself that I was getting fat when I was just no longer a kid.

"You're dumb; you're gross; you're ugly; you're fat. You're weird; you're stupid." Who would like someone like that, was what I thought?

And when I walked around saying it to myself, thinking those things to myself, how could I even fathom liking myself? I was worse to myself than I was to my made-up enemies. I would laugh at my dreams. I was undeserving, average, uninteresting, and nothing special. I was a B student, and the material didn't stick despite working so hard. Even now, learning new things takes a conscious effort for me not to get frustrated.

At that age, I requested my first gym membership for Christmas. It wasn't about being healthy. It was about stopping the development of the curves that I was starting to show. This began years of unhealthy, restrictive dieting and unproductive workouts while talking down to myself. This was the beginning of hating myself into a new person. I continued this cycle for twenty long years. Shit-talking myself and telling myself awful things.

I was saying things I would never say to another human.

"I'm stupid."

'I'm fat."

"I'm disgusting."

"I am a mess."

I was using these words repeatedly. I was making them my reality, which became how I saw myself for a long time.

High school became one big game of "how small, and unseen can I stay?" It was much easier that way.

"Nobody will think anything about me if they can't see me. I have a couple of friends and my family. That was all I wanted or needed, and even though one of the two friends wasn't very nice to me, she was consistently there, so she got to stay. I didn't need or want to join clubs or sports teams. That would just be me trying to be seen again.

I would wear baggy pajama pants and hoodies and rarely do my hair and makeup. "I am not pretty anyways. What's the point? Why try? Why would I want people to look at me?"

The times when someone new would see me, I would subconsciously self-sabotage and ruin those relationships quicker than they started.

What about dating? No way. Way too much risk involved in that. They would inevitably reject me, I thought. Remember that whole needing to be liked thing? Dating wasn't happening. I couldn't handle the idea of rejection, and I didn't believe that I was worth it, and in my mind, there was no chance of acceptance. I didn't accept myself. How could I expect anyone else to?

That is how high school went, getting through each day, getting to the next day, getting to graduation, to get out before anyone noticed I was there.

In my sophomore year, I started working in a restaurant. I was still innocent and shy, and yet, I shined. I threw myself into my job, and I don't think there has been another 16-year-old that has taken hosting that seriously since. I ran around, and I bussed the servers' tables. I ran food, and I ran the waitlist. I remember the compliments and the extra tips from servers. I was the show's star and took pride in my job.

Or was it the extra attention I got? I was able to be less invisible because everyone liked me. Everyone complimented me. I could be friends with everyone who worked there without fearing rejection. I had a group of girlfriends with the other hostesses and some of the servers. I could talk to the guys without feeling that fear of inevitable rejection. I felt safely seen. Was I safe? Not really, but people liked me, so I didn't care.

Flirtatious banter turned into going to parties at the bartender's houses. As a 16, maybe 17-year-old girl, I was introduced to alcohol and to the "hook-up" culture. I remember being that age and having the bartender (someone my naive self-considered a friend) handing me drinks from behind the bar, saying, "drink it." When I would ask what it was, I was met with a "just drink it ."I didn't drink alcohol at this point, but that whole needing approval thing had me drinking whatever they gave me (yeah…not safe).

I went to a party at that person's house once. I was 17, and he tried to get me to his room. Thankfully, I had been warned about the "line" he used to get girls by another server, and I laughed and said, "oh yeah, I heard that was your line" I walked away and returned to the party. Friends? I thought the 23-year-old man who used the same line on everyone else as me, a junior in high school, was my friend.

In the same way, I thought the 26-year-old man that would say and do whatever he felt like when he came up to the host stand was my friend. The way the cook who followed me into the cooler and blocked me in, was my friend. The way the server who walked up to me and kissed me on the back of the neck was my friend, and the way the cook who pushed me up against the wall by my neck or held on to my wrist and wouldn't let go when I told them to, were my friends. And even the food runner who would whistle whenever I walked by was my friend. Yeah...he was old enough to be my dad, too.

See, this is the thing, though. I thought these people were my friends. I didn't try to stop them. Was I uncomfortable? Sure...but that was the culture, I told myself. It was how it was at multiple restaurants I worked at. Accept it to fit in. This is what I should do to be a part of the culture. I was so focused on the fact that they gave me attention; they approved of me. And oh my gosh, they think I'm pretty? I'm good.

Respect? Who needs respect? Who cares if I disapproved of it? Who cares if I was uncomfortable with it?

At 18, I caved. I was in an industry where people worked to drink. Again, something I wasn't really into. From a young age, I was resistant to alcohol until I realized how much other people liked it.

Look how many "friends" I made when I started going to house parties and my voices that said the most horrible things to me. They began getting quieter, and I felt I could finally escape them. I was able to talk to whoever I wanted to. I fit in.

Alcohol started running the show. Just like a toxic relationship, I let it completely take control. It started innocent enough. I was drinking with my restaurant friends. Going to college, drinking was the norm there. My family drinks, too, so drinking is ok. It's me. It's normal. I thought I felt normal. I thought I fit in, finally.

Fitting in felt good. I felt safe, like I had a pack. I became obsessed with the idea of fitting in—the cool friend. I would do anything for you and party all night with you. I became the fun friend—the party girl. I could stop overthinking. I could finally chill out. I didn't have to think about every word that left my lips. Wondering if I had said the right thing. I didn't care anymore. I could finally be me, I thought. I was the opposite of myself; more on that later.

In my recent discovery of being a highly sensitive person, I have also come across some sources that claim that alcohol abuse is common in HSPs because, without realizing it, they are numbing all of the noises and feelings that can easily overstimulate them.

Away from Home

I went away to college, and I made some fantastic friends. My two current best friends came from college. I also met many people I don't talk to anymore (many people where friendship was based around alcohol). And that's ok; that is part of my experience. Part of my journey. In college, that is where my drinking started to ramp up. I was away from anyone that would tell me to stop, and I was around people my age. It was the first time we were all on our own. We could all do whatever we wanted, whenever we wanted.

I quickly went from a sweet, innocent little girl to an invisible teenager to a party girl. Looking back, I was not keeping up well, but I thought I was doing great! I was cool; I could talk to guys and get out of my head. I was becoming a part of the world, and best of all, people liked me.

I started giving myself away, letting people take from me whatever they wanted. Mind and spirit, anyway. My body, not so much yet. That came later. However, if you wanted to take up space in my mind, it was yours. Or you want to use my wings so you can fly...here you go. If it was my light you wanted, so you could shine brighter...Take it; I don't need it anyways.

The Young Adult

These habits continued through 4 years of college and then through the rest of my 20s. I wanted to party. I described myself as a social butterfly, the opposite of a homebody. On my first date with my husband, I told him, "The worst thing you could say to me is that you are a homebody."(Spoiler alert...I am the biggest homebody you have ever met).

Also, that was my worst trait?! The worst I could find was someone who didn't want to go out drinking all the time. Because that's what it was, you know, for me. I wasn't a social butterfly. I was a girl trapped in a war in her mind that wanted to drink it all away. I was a girl who couldn't stay home because that meant sitting with myself fully.

More on the hubby in a bit, before him, I spent time on rocky seas in my dating life. When I did date, I would love to make them happy. If they're happy, you're happy. I would tell myself I should be thankful anyone like them would want you. Let them say what they want. Give them all your mind, spirit, and body too. This would lead to a streak of dating controlling men. Let them do what they want. That continued through my young and mid 20's. I would notice it quickly and leave after a month or so. I remember I would say, "If this is love, then I don't want to be in love." I also used to say that some people are destined for true love, and others are supposed to be alone. Maybe I am just supposed to be alone.

I was half right, while now I have the most incredible husband, and I consider myself so lucky and so blessed to be sharing this life with him; even his love could not replace my self-love. I will tell you all more of our story together and how we fell in love, along with my love story with myself, after I finish telling you the rest of the "lost years".

As I continued drinking to stop my emotions, I realized what I was doing with all of it was numbing. When people would compliment me, I would feel good enough, numbing the voice that told me I wasn't. When I would starve myself or put myself on restrictive diets, I would feel like I had control of my weight, which I based so much of my worth on. This would numb the feeling of being fat or unattractive (because those went hand and hand for me). Also, on the flip side, I would emotionally binge eat, numbing whatever emotion I didn't want to feel that way - insert weight gain - insert shame and guilt - insert big messy cycle.

Then insert alcohol - the one that shuts it all off. That is the problem, though. Alcohol was tricky - it did "shut it off". It did "stop" the voice and numb my pain. Alcohol also shut off my joy and happiness, innocence, and brilliance (yes, I am brilliant, despite what I used to say to myself). And it was only temporary. Those feelings would return, leaving me running for another vice - another way to numb. Alcohol took the messy cycle I was living in and lit it on fire, and it halted my growth right in its tracks.

Ok, now we get back to when my love life took a turn for the right. I met Ryan in 2018. First, he is the best; he's fantastic and a prominent part of my story. As lost as I was when we met, I still found the most amazing life partner, or perhaps he found me. All that I know is I am so grateful we found each other. He saw me as this version of me long before I was this version of me. When we met, I immediately felt like I knew him, and he felt he knew me. We had a whirlwind romance, and I started running on his love…his compliments. I fell in love, and I thought I was happy. I was happy for a little bit. It was a false happiness, and I ran on his happiness. I had this constant stream of telling me I was beautiful and unique and felt accepted and loved.

Soon though, my voice telling me I wasn't good enough for him crept back in. He is a saint for loving me in my cheerful and gloomy days and constantly reminding me that I was and am good enough. My husband supports me in all ways, and that is beautiful. He supports my growth, decisions, sensitivity, and love. Even with his support, I needed to learn how to love myself.

Self-love is the source of all love, and at the start, I still had no love for myself. Running on someone else's love will never be sustainable, no matter how much that person loves and sees and understands you (or accepts it when they don't understand). I chose a supportive partner, and it is so beautiful to always have someone in my corner, and I now know I must love myself to keep my light lit.

Ryan proposed on a ski lift in Park City, Utah, in December of 2019. Yes, it was risky proposing on a ski lift, and no, he didn't drop my ring. We had talked about getting married and had picked a venue. We decided on a September 2020 wedding. I booked all the vendors, and then Covid. So, you can guess how that September wedding worked out. We continued our plans as long as possible, having people tell us, "It has to be cleared up by September" and "You will be fine," so we stayed optimistic.

At the end of July, we decided to postpone. My wedding shower was four days away, and we were having the bridal party over for an outdoor pool party after. We decided to pull off a surprise wedding, which we did, and it was magical. And everyone LOVED it. We loved it. It was a great day. Until I got hammered and fell asleep on my parent's kitchen floor. I woke up drunk the following day and decided to continue the party with the leftover champagne, Mimosas!

I gave myself all the excuses and multiple reasons why I got wasted and deserved to party. I had learned to make myself my victim, so that is what I did.

"I am covid bride. I deserve to party."

"After the week and year, I had, I wanted to do that."

"My life is crazy, and I wanted to take the edge off."

And then, I continued this path through the rest of 2020. I was drinking to stop the world and numb it all out. Covid, politics, postponed wedding planning, and feeling like I had no idea who I was anymore.

The Awakening
In December 2020, I got my wake-up call. This is what people refer to as the rock bottom moment. During a girls' weekend in Wisconsin, I got completely shit-faced. This was day two of the weekend, and night one had already started with a dinner and night out that I didn't remember the end of. I started with a Bloody Mary at breakfast, a few drinks while we were shopping, and back home after shopping and pre-gaming for dinner with an entire bottle of wine—more wine at dinner, then a bar where shot after shot of tequila started happening.

I was out of my mind (which wasn't out of the ordinary for me; that was what was normal at this point). We got back to the hotel from the bar after all day, and I wanted to continue drinking. The old me didn't know how to stop the party. The current me that knows we require 8-

9 hours of sleep is so sad for this former version of me that liked to drink into the morning hours. Anyways, I tried to walk to the hotel bar myself and got lost on the way back. Mind you, I have no memory of this; I was no stranger to putting myself in super risky situations and getting lucky that someone was watching over me. So, after getting lost, I got back and argued. At one point in the argument, I picked up a knife and threatened to use it on myself. This wasn't the first time I said and did things like this. However, it was the most intense and the most serious. I was escalating. I was so upset. The police were called, and I went voluntarily to the hospital overnight.

I vaguely remember being in the police car, and I don't remember getting to the hospital or being evaluated. I remember that the police officer was younger than I was, 30 at the time. He was nice, and you could tell he was in the profession because he wanted to help people. He tried to help me. So anyways, I woke up the next day in the hospital room with the officer still there. I was still intoxicated, but back to the point that I could have a conversation, I would remember. I was talking to him, and he was talking to me like I was real. He thanked me because of how cooperative I was. I remember him telling me many times, "You're cool." I also remember laughing and being calm at the regular hospital. He kept telling me I was waiting on a transfer and would go to a treatment center, where I would be evaluated before I could be released.

Another officer showed up at the hospital at one point, and they were talking, and he came in and talked to me. I remember he was nice too, but I felt more judgment from him. I felt like he was talking to me more like a cop and less like a companion, which was good to have too. I remember asking the original officer why he had to stay at the hospital with me, and he gave me this look, and I answered my question and said, "oh, yeah. I guess what I said and did last night means I cannot be left alone." He smiled and nodded. "Sorry," I sheepishly said, turning over to fall asleep.

So, the transfer vehicle to the treatment center came, and I hopped in. The ride to the treatment center was about an hour away, and as I said before, I thought I was being evaluated, and then I thought my husband would come to get me. It was a Sunday morning, and when I got there, I was sitting at the desk checking in, and they told me I had to stay overnight. Even as I type this, my chest feels panicky and constricted. I was still not all the way sober at this point. It was 9 am. They told me I had to stay overnight, and I lost it.

I panicked and was so scared, and I remember telling the person who worked the front desk that "I had never been in trouble before." She kindly said to me, "you are not in trouble." That is still what I was worried about. Being in trouble, what other people thought. They took my clothes, phone, and wedding ring to prevent theft. I was terrified. I was embarrassed. I was in a situation I had somehow avoided for longer than I should have. I called my husband, and I was freaking out, crying and shaking, saying, "they're saying I have to stay overnight. I can't do this." He was amazing and reassured me that everything would be ok, telling me that I was in a safe place and that I could use the time to rest.

So dressed in my hospital clothes, I walked back to my room with a cot in it, and I was able to take a nap, and when I woke up to a knock at my door. "Lunch is here," one of the residents told me. "Ok, thanks," I said as I turned over and fell back asleep.

When I woke up again, I grabbed my paper dixie cup to fill it with water, and a chicken sandwich was sitting there for me. It was a frozen chicken patty sandwich with a packet of mayo sitting next to it. I can still taste it. I ate it, grateful that I could eat. One of the residents sat down, talked to me, and asked me why I was there, so I told her my story the night before. She said, "well, at least you are sitting here and not the county jail," and then she told me about her life, how she had been there for years, how her husband had died, and how heroin was her drug of choice. At that moment, I realized that these residents had heavy addictions, and I wasn't feeling judgmental toward them. I was relating to them, feeling what they were feeling, and feeling like them.

After eating and conversing, I went back to my room and sat on my bed. There was a common sitting area outside, but I couldn't be there. The lady that worked the front desk (she was an earth angel) came back to my room. She told me that my family had been calling and trying to get me released since I got there. She let me use her cell phone to talk to my family. She was trying to help me get out. I asked her what would happen if I just left, .and she said, "you would have a warrant out for your arrest."

She had no power to release me, but she was instrumental in helping me. She looked at me like she knew I had learned, like I was going to change; she knew I could go home. That woman was so fantastic. She finally told me they could call the police station that placed the hold on me and release it. So about 5 hours into my stay, she returned and said the police wanted to evaluate me over the phone. So, she brought me into a room where I talked to the police, and they asked me a series of questions. Then they had me blow into a breathalyzer. At 2 pm the next day, I blew a .05. Again, the employee vouched for me, and I was released when my husband came to get me. Walking out of that place after 7 hours felt like seven days.

I was crushed. I felt like I had let everyone down. I let myself down. In my mind, the whole point of life was to be fun and for people to like me, and I was doing the opposite. I knew it was time to do something. While at the time, this felt like the worst day of my life, it was the best thing that could have happened at the time. I had been numb, asleep, and unaware. And here was my wake-up call.

This was my chance to change, and I knew it. It was time to start the comeback story. I knew I would stop drinking for a while. Six months was the amount of time I gave myself. I thought that would be enough to rebuild, to heal. I thought healing was something I could do fast, and part of that was true, and I also started learning how deep some of the wounds, most of which were self-inflicted, I had. It was time to change. I didn't quite know how I was going to do it. I still didn't know how to give myself love.

What I did know was I was finally ready to fight for myself. My older brother asked me if I wanted a storywork coach. I said yes. Without realizing it, this was the first time in a long time I said yes to myself. I entered coaching and stopped drinking for six months. Welcome to my first big shift. Coaching is amazing. Shout out to the Enlifted coaching community, and Mark England, the head coach and my first coach (since then, I have worked with three different Enlifted certified coaches as a client and became certified myself).

Mark taught me so much about words, about how I was using them, and I was using my words against me. I learned the power of language, breath, and the strength I already held within myself, and I started using those powers. I walked into coaching feeling broken, and by the first session, I was empowered and ready to take my life back.

I started creating the me I wanted to be and, in many ways, the me I used to be. I learned about myself and started learning many of the topics this book outlines. I learned tools that I had used every day since.

The Revert

I did start drinking again in July of 2021 (I only planned for a six-month hiatus at first), and I began to slip very soon after that. I held on to the tools as much as possible, and then I remembered how easy it was to shut my feelings off.

I started ignoring the awareness that I had worked so hard to create. I was still in a better place mentally but was beginning to numb again. As I attempted to numb my feelings, I was turning away from my intuition. I was returning to my pattern of the fun friend who wanted to party, which happened *fast.*

We had our big wedding, which was another beautiful and magical day. We loved our day and got to have the party, and I remember being relieved that I was no longer a pandemic bride and no longer planning our wedding. We went on our honeymoon, my sister-in-law got married a month before our second wedding, and we did a dual honeymoon with them. That was fun.

By this point, I was turning back into the party girl, the fun friend. I thought I had more of a hold on it, but that wasn't true. I was drinking to the point of not remembering the night before, and I look back now and know that I was drinking to stop the overstimulating parts of my environment again.

Ian

I have a little brother too. He is four years younger, and his name is Ian, and he is the best, the most amazing blend of hilarious and wise. Ian was like my shadow growing up. Many summers were spent playing in the yard with our two neighbors.

Since we were young kids, through college, Ian and I were together a lot. I went away to school, and Ian was in high school at the time. He came and visited me a few times in school, and he was always a big hit. I remember I used to introduce him like this: "This is my little brother Ian, my favorite person."

Then in November 2021, Ian passed away suddenly. I will never forget the phone call, the day, how my body felt after that, and how my mind clouded. The way the world changed that day. How I felt for months that I was living in a nightmare, and I was going to wake up, and it would not be real. I remember the way it felt like grief was swallowing me up. We felt like a rug had been pulled out from underneath us. We spent a lot of time together as a family after that, which was beautiful how we all came together and how our loved ones gathered around us and supported us while we grieved.

A friend to many, the best advice giver, the hilarious and most perfectly timed and delivered jokes. A sweetness, a willingness to have honest conversations, and an outrageous love for dogs. The BEST speech writer and deliverer and an all-around legend. Intelligent, hardworking and the life of the party, and a person that walks into the room and automatically lifts it. That is what I remember Ian as.

Right after, I was feeling were so blurry, and I already felt off balance. I spent most of my time with my family. At first, I didn't want to be intoxicated. I didn't want to feel any more out of my body than I already did. I would have a few drinks, but not more than 1 or 2. At first, I didn't want to feel any more fuzzy-headed than the shock had me feeling.

Then about a week later, I caught my first buzz, and the numbing took over. My body remembered how easy it was to stop my brain from thinking. I was in the past, imagining a new future, and all the emotions overwhelming. I continued using alcohol as a crutch and as something I was using to stop my brain from thinking. I was full of numbness. So, after six months of some high highs and many low lows, I was full-on drinking myself into shutting off again.

The Reset

I thought, "ok, I will participate in dry January. I will reset it and be good to go after that. I lasted two weeks.

On January 15th, I went out to lunch, and I drank. Then when we got home from lunch, I continued to drink, went out for a friend's birthday, and I continued to drink wine. Not only did I choose to break the January commitment I had made, but I also chose to do it in a "drink all day" fashion.

I got drunk, I stayed up late, and I got emotional. I felt feelings that wanted to come out in an inauthentic way. On the 16th, I woke up to the worst "Sunday Scaries." What a cute name we give to something that could also be described as crippling anxiety. I couldn't get out of bed. My heart was racing, and I was sweating.

My intuition and the tools I had learned in coaching almost automatically kicked back that next day. I realized where I was, and I am so thankful for all my work that helped me see it— (TGFE - Thank God for Enlifted).

"What am I doing, and who am I turning back into?" I thought to myself. And I didn't love the answer.

So, I decided to be done, this time for good. I remembered being present and aware and realized how much better I liked that feeling than the zombie effect that the booze "gave" me. As we have discussed, I have now learned that I was made to feel everything all the way through without shutting it off or numbing. As painful as some of the things I thought at this time were, I was supposed to feel it. And as I felt it, I could move with the emotions. While there will always be a lot of feelings, as I feel them, a resolution for myself does come along with that.

I stopped drinking on January 16th, 2022, and threw myself into myself. I used all the tools I had learned and started building my life for myself. I started looking at what I wanted again. I started seeing so clearly. And I realized it was never about the alcohol. It was never about the negative relationship with food, and it was never about other people's compliments.

It was about me. Those other patterns were side effects, symptoms, and conditions of fighting against myself for so long. Through this life, through these patterns, I had turned myself into my enemy. I had become a victim of myself. I was locked in this fight against myself, an all-out war in my body and mind. So, I stopped.

And I started loving myself.

That part was automatic this time. I could forgive myself and start moving forward, immediately using what I had learned previously, and I have expanded further since then.

My continued expansion has been a wonderful experience, and it is ongoing. I continued coaching through the next year with two other coaches.

Matt has been there to help me with my relationship with alcohol and, at the same time, helped me free my inner child. Matt helped me remember how creative I am and is, in turn, an essential reason for believing in myself enough to write this book.

Then there is Kimberly, who helped me work on my relationship with food and taught me to look at food as art, which is also creativity when you look at it. Kim also helped me tap into my goddess energy and how divinely powerful I am, which is also a huge reason for this book.

I worked together on my relationship with food and my relationship with alcohol, and that is where I realized how they were always the same thing. They were there to help me cope, help me survive, and help me numb.

Now I want nothing to do with numbing. I want to feel *everything* that I get to feel. That highly sensitive and over-emotional kid owned her superpower. Now that I realize that I am a highly sensitive person, and it is an innate wiring in my brain, I embrace everything I feel and authentically.

So, I took my power back. I am expanding further and further every day while living in this now. Yesterday I grew further than the day before, and today I have grown even more than yesterday. My growth and expansion have become the only destination I am searching for.

I spend at least an hour with myself when I wake up, usually 2-3 hours. I have a Zen Den set up in my closet. My Zen Den is a small closet deep enough to lie in. I have cushions, pillows on the floor, and shelves full of candles and crystals. I decorated them with different signs and tapestries. I light the candles and burn incense.

I created my own space that I come to and spend time in, listening to myself and fully connecting with myself every day. I am here now, writing my sacred story in my sacred space.

In the morning, I connect my body, mind, and soul—at least 20 minutes of meditation, a 10-minute of stretching, and 10 minutes of mind connection. My mind activities have more variance. Sometimes and most of the time recently, I write to connect with my mind. Sometimes I color or draw, and sometimes I read. The connection of the body, mind, and soul helps keep me in my Now. When all those elements work together, the push and pull that can happen with a disconnect become much less frequent. When the disconnect does happen, I immediately feel it and realize it. I have the awareness and the tools now to reconnect.

When I align these elements, my nervous system can relax. I also do at least 10 minutes of breathwork in the morning. There is an entire chapter on breathing later because intentional breathing is essential. Without learning to control my breath, there is no chance I could have healed myself as far as I have.

Then I go for a walk. Walking is so simple and so magical. Most of my magic has been found in simple activities and changes.

Before, I would complicate things and try to manipulate, control, and regulate everything. Now I can set goals and achieve them as a byproduct of the way I am living, and if something happens in my life that redirects me, I can adjust without beating myself up and instead loving myself.

I also have the awareness that surrender, and allowance are essential. Where I used to fight against myself or fight against certain feelings, now I can let them be there and love them no matter what they are, knowing that every moment is a crucial part of me. Every moment means something if you let it.

There is so much I can share and want to share. Because we all have this power already to become who we want to be. Once we realize how much beauty and amazement this life offers, grabbing onto it becomes the greatest opportunity. It becomes automatic.

You become automatic. That is my journey with myself. Everyone is different. Everyone's entire story is different. We all have our superpowers. And they are all already within us. This was my story, the rest of this book is to show you how I got to this point where I love every moment, and if you choose to expand into your own Now, it is to help you write yours.

Chapter 2:
Realization

When you look in the mirror
What is it that you see?
Chains and shackles
Or are you free?

Your life is your choice
it is up to you
you get to choose
how you move through

Do you build on each day
and live in this time?
Or do you only look forward
and back behind?

See, your life is right here
it is happening right now
Understanding is not important
Don't worry about how

You can look up at the sky
And know you are guided along
And then look in your heart
and see you are strong

You have learned some lessons

Some were hard
You have lived through some things
You may even be scarred

So, take a good look
down deep inside
and know there is nothing
you need to hide

Start to see the moment
and live for your soul
Everything is already inside you
and you already know

Meet yourself where you are right now. Stay in your body and listen to yourself. Because that is how you see it, that is how you see yourself. That's how you stay here; that's how you learn to be. The answers you are looking for are already inside of you. I had been searching for external validation and solutions for so long, and once I realized that everything was in me, the responses showed up so clearly. I know now that the only person that needs to accept me is me, I do not need to be understood, and I do not need to understand. I am here to love and be loved.

At first, when I started healing, my words sounded like "I can't keep living this way" and "This is not who I am." Then when I entered coaching, I learned the power of speaking in affirmations instead of negations. Unlearning certain parts of you that are untrue to who you are, is essential, and we will get there in the chapter titled "Unlearn." First, it is crucial to look inside yourself.

Who do you want to be? How can you become that person?

What CAN you do if you can't keep living this way? If this is not who you are, then who ARE you? Or who do you want to create? I learned to live for myself and to make myself my priority. As I mentioned in my story, it took work for me. I'd work out, go for walks, attend coaching sessions, and fix toxic relationships with food, alcohol, and mainly myself before I thoroughly learned how to stay in my moments. It is also important to note that while healing takes time, the mindset can be changed immediately. You can start living in this moment, in this exact moment.

People told me that I couldn't change overnight, and I would challenge that. You can change overnight. Many mornings I wake up feeling completely transformed from the person I was before. I embrace that. It is so beautiful to know that I can create myself repeatedly. I hold my power, and I get to decide who I want to be, and in 15 minutes, if I learn something new or am presented with a new path, I can recreate myself again.

Shifts may happen over and over. For example, you may be experiencing a significant realization, and as you read this, the lightbulb could go on.

Likely, though, since you have reached for this book, you did so because you have already had a moment like that. So, congratulations. Let's continue the expansion and grow together. Be open to more shifts as you read this book. Be open to seeing new pathways and be open to taking those.

The feeling that there is more, that you are more, is real. You can be who you want to be, that person is already inside of you, and they are yours to create. You were born with everything you need to succeed into the person you want to be. The key is living life for the moment instead of the achievements.

If you do this, you will naturally create the person you want to be when you stop looking forward and start looking inward. The achievements will come, and you will realize that the true magic is in all the moments and learning to feel them all.

The realization is often called a shift, an awakening, or a transformation. I am partial to the word expansion. The term expansion is continuous. Instead of only allowing yourself one big moment that opens your eyes, you can keep going and keep opening your eyes and your heart wider and wider. Expansive moments are those places in time when you realize that you want to start living as the genuine and authentic you and when you learn more about who that authentic you is and begin to embody that you.

Sometimes expansion can come after a wake-up call, or it can come due to burnout or anxiety. They can also come as a gift from someone on your path. All three coaches mentioned initially have gifted me with expansive moments and ideas.

Expansion can come out of nowhere like it is dropped into your lap. When you feel it, you will know, and you are ready. Being ready is not something you feel. Being "ready" is something you choose. So, are you choosing to be ready? Are you ready to choose to start living as the true you? Is that the choice you are going to make?

So, let's back up. What can you do? Who do you want to be? Take a few minutes before you continue. I will provide you with a space on the next page to write your answers right in the book. If you have a journal that you keep, put your answer there. *You are writing these words down, meaning they are way more likely to happen.*

Write here:

Realizations are different for everyone, you may have one big moment, or you may have many little things happen that lead to your expansions. You will also likely have many transformations as you grow and expand. Remember, you will sometimes feel different from one day to the next. That is a beautiful thing because it means if we want to be somewhere else or someone else, we can transform right here and now, over and over again. Some people see that as scary, and that is ok. Fear is not a blockage. Fear should propel you because usually, when you move through something you are fearful of, you are expanding yourself even further.

Start here, now. When it comes down to it, that is all you have, the moment you are in. Are you living in a way in which that thought is comfortable, or does that feel heavy? Is there something you would change? There are memories that you carry, and there are thoughts of the future that may wander in. Still, though, all you can touch, all you physically have is this moment you are in. Grab onto it and feel it. Fall in love with it because the moment is already in love with you.

The moment you're in is amazing, and you will soon be able to see all that each moment offers you. Once you see that every single experience in this life holds beauty, the expansion will feel effortless. There are the obvious beautiful moments, of course. Celebrations include weddings, birthdays, new friendships, and beautiful love stories. It is essential to know and hold onto the fact that painful moments also have so much beauty. Every hardship is something you can grow through. And when you believe that you start to be able to see fully that beauty that is in all the moments. Some of my most extensive experiences come after what feels like crushing pain. In those moments, I learn so much about myself, and after I learn so much about myself, I can recognize what is me and what is not. Then I can let the patterns I have been learning my whole life dissolve away.

We are used to hearing phrases like "tomorrow is a new day" when experiencing a painful or gloomy day. Here is the thing, *today* is the moment we're in. We slip out of that moment when we give up on today and start living for tomorrow. We give away that moment. How many moments are you willing to give away, to bypass, to get to tomorrow? There were lessons to be learned and beauty to see. Instead of experiencing it, we skip those moments and move into tomorrow because we tell ourselves tomorrow will be better. What if it is not better? Will you give tomorrow away to the next tomorrow, then?

We must stop losing the moments. We are meant to be here for all of them, learning from all of them. We must feel. I am highly sensitive and an empath, so I know that some feelings feel like they are too much. And as I have learned to sit with those emotions, I have learned that my power is in the feeling, and my sensitivity is fantastic.

Allow yourself to feel it all. Any feeling felt all the way through is a good feeling.

Let's talk about the RAS. The reticular activating system, among many other functions, acts as a filter for your brain. It determines what you see and what fades into the background. The RAS can be trained. If you are living as your victim, you will look for the ugly, the scary and the things that block you. When you start looking at the good, the RAS starts to recognize that change. It takes practice, like any skill, and also like any skill, once you practice enough, it becomes effortless. Soon your RAS will have you looking for what is beautiful, calming, and the things that free you, and before you know it, that will become automatic.

Learning to see the beauty in all things is so important and unique because it allows us to be right where we are. Knowing that pain comes with beauty makes it easier to sit with painful moments instead of skipping through them to get back to what is easy. If you know that there is growth, a lesson, or a form of beauty at that moment, you will choose to stay there to experience that expansion. You take back your power by staying where you are. The pain will feel less daunting, and eventually, there will even be a sense of excitement because you will know what is coming from the pain.

Remember, joy and love are a state of being. Even when the days are painful or sad, you are still loved and joyful. Emotions are not on a hierarchy. No feeling is better than the other. They are neutral. It is a gift to get to experience all emotions. It is a gift to articulate how you are feeling and be aware of what it is and how your body reacts. It is the most significant gift to become joy and love in a way that protects you and allows you to feel them all as they come.

A key piece within your realization stage will be learning that to stay in the moment, your priority and focus should be on the journey instead of the destination. It is important to remember that life is based on your journey. Living in a destination-based mindset will have you always trying to achieve the next level instead of staying where you are and enjoying the Now. The beauty is in the moments along the journey. Living for a destination can have the effect of constantly asking yourself..." now what?" after each achievement.

Destination-based living looks like this: Goal for a teenager: Graduate high school - next step, college. Graduate college - next step, job. Job - next step, promotions. Promotions - next step, get married. Get married - the next step, buy a house. Buy a house - next step, kids. Kids - next step, promotion. Kids and promotion - next step, bigger house.

The cycle continues until retirement, and then we are so focused on living for destinations that we cannot relax and enjoy our retirement. Not to mention we spent all the moments we had in most of our years living for future destinations.

Live for the journey—set goals, of course. Learn from the past, of course. That is part of the human experience, and then live your life in a way where you know everything in the past brought you to now, the most beautiful and authentic version of you. Live your life in a way where you currently live as the you that has achieved your goals. Health, success, and happiness will become effortless.

The realization is the place where writing is critical. Well, one of the many places where writing is vital. At this moment, it is time to get curious. Get curious about what has been standing in your way. Take a second now (next page provided for space) and journal. How does the version of you that you want to be live?

What actions can you take in the present to live as that person? What steps can you take to become that person? What is the identity of that person? What do they like? What do they do? What habits do they create for themselves? What makes them feel alive, and what gives them purpose? What has stopped you from being able to propel yourself? What is preventing this moment that you're in from being exactly where you want to be?

Write those things down, too, and read them out loud. These are the stories that make you. These are the stories that have created you. Get them out of your head and put them on paper. Look at them and see how you have been living. Is this how you want to live? Is this what you want to do? If not, what do you want to change? Act right here at this moment. Write those out.

Write here:

Once you realize this way of living, you will free yourself of the chains connecting you to the past and the worries of the future, and you can start focusing on the person you want to be right now.

Get a journal, get a calendar, and help yourself become that person by simply scheduling what would get you there into your days. Start speaking to yourself as though you are already the person who achieved those goals. You will believe in your capabilities, and before long, the wins along the way will be a by-product of how you live. And trust me when I say there will be a lot of wins.

Our life is made up of the stories that we tell ourselves. Anxiety, sadness, busyness, manipulation, or trauma can be some of the stories.

Where are these stories coming from? Likely, from stories of your past or stories of your present.

Write these down too. Write down what is blocking you. Because it is a story, you are telling yourself repeatedly. And a story in your head is stuck, a story written down is freed. Study those stories. What are you feeling? Where are you feeling it? Have you felt this feeling before? When was the first time, and has this become a pattern in your life that you now identify as a personality trait or a common issue?

Write here:

How can we rewrite the story? How can you find what is purely you versus what is your pattern? More on patterns in chapter three. One of the biggest realizations you can have is when you know that you want something different for yourself, and then you realize that it is possible and necessary for you to shift something in your life to become that person. You are ready to transform because you have decided to be prepared.

Like me, your realization will likely start when you see how you have been fighting against parts of yourself instead of loving yourself. Then you will begin to realize that you have the power within you. Self-love is the source of all love. You will see that sentence more than once in this book, and it will be a recurring theme.

The cliche "you can't pour from an empty cup" is spot on. Once you know that love is not something you do and that love is a state of being, expansion can happen. You have to love yourself to expand because you have to love yourself to be willing to sit with yourself and listen deeply.

How do you feel when you hear the word emotion? Are you avoidant or reluctant to feel? Are you scared to show the way you are feeling? Are you afraid of feeling the pain all the way through? Do you allow yourself to celebrate your wins in life? Feeling your feelings is paramount.

Hear this; any emotion felt all the way is a "good" emotion. Feeling your emotions all the way through is the only thing that makes them suitable. Emotions are neutral. Humans are the ones that have assigned the title of good or bad to emotions. Part of being in the moment you're in is being willing to feel what is there. If you can feel it, you can heal it. It is essential to take the hierarchy of emotions humans create down and realize and embrace that all you feel is there for your growth.

Part of being in the moment you're in is being willing to feel what is there. I just said that, and even my original words minimized it. Did you grow up thinking that showing emotions was weak? When I was a kid, I felt so much, I was a profoundly feeling child who grew into an adult who finally learned that her sensitivity was her superpower, and it took a lot of work to get here.

Being so sensitive as a child was hard to understand for me and those around me. I couldn't always make sense of my feelings, and being over-emotional seemed like such an inconvenience, like I was wasting everyone's time.

I was often told I was highly sensitive, over-emotional, or fragile. I remember the words "let it go" ringing loudly, but I didn't know how to let things go. So instead of letting them go, I tried to turn the feelings off. I tried to cope with them in whatever way I could.

Emotional eating, telling myself I didn't matter, and eventually drinking. Whatever could shut that emotion off, I would try because they seemed wrong.

Part of my realization was that every time I cut an emotion off, I buried it deep inside myself. And as I had that past emotion holding me back, I could never be in the present. I had way too many unresolved feelings.

Pushing emotions down didn't work. I had all this pent-up emotion that I needed to feel; I was made to feel. This is where the storywork coaching I went into after the hospital played a part in my healing. I went into the past, I found those "stuck stories," and I wrote them down and got them out of my head and on paper, where I could see them, and I read them, and I read them with breath. I realized the past was my stories, my responsibility (not necessarily my fault or anyone's fault, and now I got to be the owner of them). I healed a lot of unresolved traumas. I made a solid plan to move forward, and I started living day by day, and soon enough, I was living moment by moment.

Realize now that the fact that we get to feel is beautiful. Everything that is there, every emotion, every tear, every sensation in your body. They are supposed to be there. They are teaching us something, and they are helping us grow.

Realize also that you are allowed to feel. You are allowed to be hurt, and you are allowed to cry. You are entitled to feel like nobody understands your emotion, and you are allowed not to understand everyone else's emotions.

You are on your journey in this life. Everyone else is on a different journey, and just as we don't want other people influencing us unwillingly, we don't need to force everyone to see the world our way, either. This is something I have recently realized too. If you are so busy focusing on other people's journeys, how can you be in the moment on your own?

Trust yourself to feel. Trust yourself to know because you do. You already know. This may feel like a lot right now but stick with me. By the end of this book, you will see that feeling that is there will help you be free. Trying to skip feelings causes us to miss the moments, so if you take one thing from this chapter, let it be this word.

Feel.

And once you set yourself free, you will be so aware of your moment; you will be able to feel when you are out of your moment, and you will know how to bring yourself back into this moment.

Discover the true you versus what is a pattern that you learned along the human experience. Discover what your ego is and what your soul is. Awareness of the patterns is critical in the awakening of your true self.

Even though the patterns are not the true you, we are going to love them, and we are going to see them; your patterns are a part of your human story. The patterns want to be loved and accepted. They likely have even helped you to get here to the moment you're in.

Chapter 3:
Patterns

Who did you want to be
before the world grabbed hold?
Have you learned who you are
Or what you have been told?

See, there is more inside.
then a heart and a brain
You're taught to be sunshine.
When you are allowed to be rain

See, you walk through this world.
Picking up things that you've learned
Hearing not to get too close to fires,
Because they will leave you burned

So, you stay far away.
Even when the weather turns frigid
and you'll start to learn
you are living too rigid.

They will say
that fire can scorch you,
but there are times.
when it can also rescue

We learn these lessons.

What is good, and what is bad?
We learn it is better
to be happy than sad

So we always walk around
with a smile on our face
while our heart turns
to a dark and cold place

It's ok to feel that way.
As long as they don't know.
so, put on a smile
and don't let the hurt show.

Soon you will learn.
Faking it is the only way.
And you've be lying to others.
Then yourself every day

Let go of the patterns.
Conditions you were taught
Put trust in yourself.
In the web you'll be uncaught

What parts of you are you? What were you born with? What is your most authentic version? Because as we move through the world, we pick up patterns. Personality traits that are described as "just the way you are," may be patterns. Remember our discussion on stories in the last chapter? Patterns are the result of the stories we tell ourselves over and over. Patterns can also result from conditioning from your environment and the people around you. More on that later in this chapter. While many people mistake patterns as characteristics, they were often assigned to you and ingrained in you until you believed they were a part of you. They are not purely you. Once you become aware of the pattern and you see the pattern, you can gain a sense of freedom. The pattern may still exist and pop up, and you will know what to do. You will be able to tell the difference.

There are many different patterns you can hold and identify as yourself. Without the awareness of them or the willingness to explore them and allow them to be there, many people walk through life on autopilot, believing that their patterns are their true identities. Patterns can be egoic, conditional, and inauthentic to your higher purpose.

The list of patterns is endless. Some examples include people-pleasing (a big one of mine), being short-tempered, having addictive personalities, being easily distracted, and codependency. We develop patterns as we grow, which can come from a few places.

Some patterns come from places of doing what we did when we learned to survive. I developed a people-pleasing habit when I realized that other people's happiness came before mine and that it was more important to be well-liked than treated well. As innocent as these patterns may have started, they became harmful later in my life. I became so obsessed with people liking me, or the fear that they wouldn't, that I let myself be treated very unsafely. I lost the ability to set boundaries and protect myself.

The way we talk to ourselves matters in so many ways. Pattern development is affected by our self-talk. When I spent time telling myself I was different than everyone else and that nobody cared what I had to say, I created, or at least continued, a pattern of being shy and sweet. I identified as meek and timid. I was making that reality with what I was saying to myself. That is not who I am. That was a direct result of what I said to myself.

Also, negative self-talk itself can be a pattern. A pattern that leads to more patterns. Now, this is getting more complex.

If you start telling yourself from a young age that you are not good enough, you will create a pattern of continuing to say and eventually believing you are not. This pattern will keep you thinking you are not good enough. You will look for why you are not good enough and reinforce the belief. The truth is, though, you have always been good enough. Hear those words when you read them. You were born good enough. The patterns are not you, and you can drop them and let them dissolve.

As a young child, you may have received praise when putting others before yourself or been labeled thoughtful, caring, or kind. Making others smile and feeling their happiness may have taught you that others' happiness comes before your own. It is hard to learn the importance and necessity of self-love when you constantly strive and make it a mission to lift everyone else up. This can cause you to empty your cup, trying to fill others' cups first. You learn that you should smile even when you have a bad day. You are taught to be polite to everyone, even if they creep you out. Later in life, this could cause you to put yourself second in relationships or allow toxic behavior or abuse just because someone compliments or tells you they love you. Knowing that it is ok and necessary to put yourself first is essential. You are always your priority.

One more example of a conditioned pattern could be something you stopped doing due to other people's words or thoughts about it. Something you loved.

Did you love singing as I did? Did you love a particular sport? Did you love drawing or painting? Did you love all those things at one point? Did people tell you that your dream was too big or that would be hard to achieve? When you were met with resistance, were you encouraged to stop doing what you were doing and try something different? Over time this can become a pattern too. Stopping when things get hard and staying in your comfort zone. This is a pattern that can halt growth and expansion right in its tracks.

So, think back now. What did you love to do as a child? Did you stop because you lost the love, or when you think about it, is there still a part of you that loves that idea? Did you stop because someone told you were not good at it? Or did you stop because someone told you wouldn't pay the bills? Again, this may not have come from a malicious place from the person on the other end of the conversation, and yet it may have caused you to give up doing something you loved before you even had to think about the money.

Take another minute to write. Write out the things you loved to do as a kid and who you wanted to be, the things that felt amazing at first and then felt like too big of a dream to achieve. The things that made the hours feel like minutes.

In the space on the next page, list those out and see if you missed anything. Anything you turned away from to get to the next destination? What can you reconnect with to reconnect to your inner child? They are still there.

Write here:

How we grow up has a lot to do with who we become. That is a part of being a human being. What if the point is to avoid becoming anything? What if we are here to learn to be? To feel? *To experience the moment, we are in?* This brings me full circle, back to another place we visited previously. Another area that can breed patterns and that is putting the emphasis on the destinations instead of the journey.

Destination-focused living is another common reason for pattern development. When looking toward the next big thing, we ignore the little things. We also may need to remember our true selves or what the universe is trying to tell us to get to our goals. What happens if we don't hit those goals? Do we think less of ourselves?

The example from earlier about becoming a workaholic for a promotion is one that we can use here again. How many promotions will there be? For most of us, that is a ladder we climb without end. So, we create this pattern of working so hard, and for what? What happens after we get the promotion? More money - what are we going to do with that money? What is the next destination we can get to? Bigger house? So, then we spent so much time focused on the house.

"If I can get that bigger house now, I will be happy."

You are then creating a pattern that bases your worth on getting to the next destination, causing being in the moment nearly impossible. Another common theme of this book... joy and happiness are not there to be found. They are a state of being and a choice you can make now. Any voices that tell you will be happy when you get to a destination, whether the house, the marriage, kids, or a goal weight, are lying to you. They are speaking from the pattern and not the accurate you. The true self knows that joy is found in each moment you're in.

Patterns are sometimes good things at certain points in our lives. They may have protected us from situations we were in repeatedly. Patterns were picked up when we were developing and learning to survive.

Now we get to become aware of and appreciate our patterns. Thank them for keeping us safe, and then allow them to dissolve. We are letting them go now to thrive.

Living with a pattern is learning to love the pattern. See, many coaches and books will teach you to fight the pattern, to combat the ego.

I will not tell you to fight against anything in this book. Fighting against myself or anyone else never worked in my healing.

I am here to tell you to stop fighting and love the patterns. Love the ego. They will be there, and as one pattern dissolves, you will likely discover more. A pattern you thought was gone may pop back up in times of high stress or heavy emotion. Remember that some of your patterns were ingrained from early childhood. See the pattern and love the pattern. That is all they want; when you give them that, they will be quiet. When you try to fight them, they will try to be louder.

Even though the patterns are not the true you, they are a part of your human experience, which means they are beautiful too. Fight against them, and they will fight back. Loving them will allow them to be your friend and allow you to live and work together in harmony. The pattern will soon realize they no longer need to be present and dissolve. Unlearn the fight.

Chapter 4:
Unlearn

Learning to unlearn
is something you will need to know.
Unlearning is something
Imperative to grow.

We were taught so much;
conditioned how to be.
We learn to reverse that
in order to be free.

All the lessons you were taught
swirling in your head
How can we move through them
and let them be dead?

It takes practice to
unlearn what you learned.
First, the need to be liked.
you have to stop the yearn.

The only person who needs to like you,
is the *you* in your spirit
Listen from inside.
I promise you will hear it.

You learn what to continue.
and know what to stop now.

You will start to see the moment.
And you will see how.

How to keep on moving
In a way that keeps you still
Listen to the inner knowing.
And know your true will.

Unlearn the false first.
Then learn what is true.
Let go of the ego.
And hang on to you.

To fly we first must let go of what weighs us down.

Sometimes when I am reading a book I often wonder about the author. What were they thinking at the time they were writing? So here I am this morning, sitting down to write, and I have been writing this book in sections, and I have been moving back and forth in these chapters writing where I am called to that day. As I meditate, new inclusions come to me. As I write, I learn more about myself.

Today unlearning is top of mind. So here I am, with bits and pieces of the next chapters completed, and knowing that there is more to add to the previous. My journey is active. Sitting down and writing this book in order would be, for me, destination-based living. Write to complete. I am writing in flow. And I have learned that it is important for me to stay in the moment I am. I, myself, have unlearned destination-based living. Writing this book is part of my journey and I am fully here in all the moments during it.

Before I continue, let me reiterate something I have said before to make myself very clear. You can love yourself right now. You can be happy right now. You do not have to learn or unlearn anything to live that truth. You only must decide.

Remember love and joy are a state of being (I am unsure how many times I have said that so far and I know it is a lot, it is important) and you can put yourself in that state in this moment, right now. Sit down. Feel where you are. Feel whatever is supporting you beneath you. Feel where that support contacts your body.

Take a deep breath and repeat "I am joy" three times slowly, breathing in between each. Take another deep breath and repeat "I am love" three times slowly, breathing in between each. How do you feel? Do you want to feel like you are made of joy and love? It really is as simple as repeating those affirmations daily. You will feel it. You will become it. Partially because you will unlearn all the patterns that had you convinced that you were anything besides those things.

Let me also make myself *very* clear on one more point. I am still unlearning, and I believe I will be unlearning for a long time. Maybe even forever. This book is not written in a linear timeline. Writing a step-by-step linear healing book would be inauthentic to me.

Healing is not linear, and life is not linear. And thank goodness for that, because a linear life would be a life spent on one path, we get to adjust. That is what makes this life so exciting, so fascinating.

Our paths change, and they are all perfect and meant for us. This book is not a step-by step how-to type book. It is a whole story of continuous actions that I live daily. These topics are my way of life, my focus, and my ways to live in the moment. They are not something you heal and move on from. They are what you want to build awareness around, and what I have built awareness around, to be able to return myself to the moment when I come out of it.

I still have moments where I jump to the future or move back into the past, and I immediately feel myself slip from the Now, and most of the time, I can put myself back there quickly these days.

I saw a perfect example of this in my life just yesterday. I will talk about feelings and emotions, how they are all good, and how we should manage our expectations in our life. We shouldn't expect certain days to feel specific ways because that is future casting.

Yesterday, I celebrated my first anniversary of being sober, and I had expectations of how I would feel. I would feel proud and accomplished and be ready to take the following steps. I would be solid, and I would be fully rebuilt and willing to take action. Well, that is true. I did feel those things.

There have been a lot of feelings I didn't expect uneasiness that has shown up in my body. I hadn't felt anxiety, fears, and feelings since I was a drinker. The shame of what I did when I did drink, and I realized that I had barely allowed those emotions to be there. And as we will discuss later, allowance is key.

I spent the year thinking how amazing I was for making the change I knew I needed to, and I am terrific for that. Taking action, especially against what you know and what you are living your life around, can be terrifying. So simply not drinking for the year was a huge accomplishment and still is a huge accomplishment. Recognizing your achievements and celebrating all your wins is essential in staying in the moment.

My one-year sober birthday was an accomplishment that came with the thought of "what's next?" or "what now?" And while it was such an empowering day, it was scary too, which threw me off. My original idea was to fight against those feelings. I know that fighting anything is counterproductive because it causes whatever we are fighting to want to fight back. I already knew this, I thought. And sometimes, we can unlearn what feels like the same lesson multiple times because it comes back up differently.

So, when those feelings came up, the initial reaction was to fight against them, and then the anxious feelings started to bubble up even worse, and because of the work I had done, it didn't take me long to realize what was going on. So, I almost immediately went to meditate went to listen to myself carefully. I was able to see where the emotion was coming from. I sat with it and allowed it to be there, knowing that it was from a pattern that wanted to be seen for a second. So instead of fighting the feelings, I turned them to love, and the anxiety subsided, and the feelings neutralized, and I noticed where they were coming from.

Love whatever is there entirely; whatever is there will love you back. Remember, too, do not expect the feeling to go away.

Sometimes the feeling doesn't go away immediately because you love it and loving your emotions only so they leave would be conditional love.

True love is unconditional. We must love whatever we feel because it is a part of our journey. Let the patterned feelings know they are genuinely seen, allowed to be there, and safe to stay inside you. It must be pure love before they feel safe to leave. To stay in your moment, allowing what is there to be there and loving it fully is imperative. Loving yourself, and anything that is a part of that self, is critical to staying in the Now.

Unlearning is important because we are unlearning the patterns and conditions we learned before. Like I said at the end of the last chapter, patterns and egos will be a part of your life. Allowing them to be there is necessary for healing. What we want to unlearn is that they are us, that they are steering the ship.

I will start with love because love is everything, and everything is love. Love is unconditional. If someone puts conditions on their love, that is not love. Now, I am not saying they didn't love you. What I am saying is love is endless, infinite, and limitless. Love does not depend on anything you do or how you are.

If you grew up and received love only when you did" something good, you may have learned that love does have conditions. Get a sound report card - receive love - you realize that love is based on your actions. Do something nice for your sibling – if someone tells you, you are a good kid and shows you love - you learn that love is only given when you are nice to others. It is ok to praise kindness and effort; it is essential to know that praise is only a tiny piece of expansive love. We are love in its purest form. We love ourselves, and then love is multiplied.

I am repeating myself here to drive this next point home. Once we unlearn that love is conditional, we can become love. We can live as love, and then giving that unconditional love becomes effortless because you will be loved, and that love will lead you and shine on to others.

This is not to say that praise is not a great thing. When getting an excellent report card, tell the child how amazing they have done and that their hard work is important. Where it can get fuzzy and confusing to that child and become harmful down the line is in attaching love to that performance.

Statements like "Oh, my gosh, you are so smart, and I love you even more now." or even "You are the best daughter/son in the whole world" after an excellent report card can condition a child to attach their worth to a report card (or whatever destination they got to). We learn that we become worth more when we get good grades or get to our next goal.

That is not true.

We have already learned that you are already worth a limitless amount. You are loved. You were born with all of that. It is already inside of you. Any teaching or conditions that love is a destination you must get to can be unlearned here and right now.

All those patterns, all those conditions. It is essential to recognize them. It is important to see what you are and what is not you. What are your conditions telling you? What is your ego telling you? What did you learn when you learned to survive?

Did you learn that money is the most important thing and that you should chase that? Did you learn that other people determine your happiness, and have you spent your life (or a lot of it) desperately chasing someone to complete you? Did you learn that your parents are the most important thing, and have you stayed codependent on them well into adulthood? Did you experience abuse or tragedy that you have tried to push down to avoid feeling hurt to protect yourself? Did you learn that emotions are wrong and that showing them makes you weak?

A huge part of staying in the moment is clearing those memories, those histories. Use them to learn and grow instead of hiding and hindering. Our memories of the past and thoughts of the future will do what they can to keep us small. Their voices will feel so loud at times. They are allowed to.

Here is what I learned, fight like hell. Fight against the normal curves that are developing in your body. Starve yourself to be skinny. Fight against yourself to get others to like you, even to the point that you hate yourself. The world seems to fight against us when we are fighting within ourselves. This is because the world is as we see it and because our world exists within us.

Everything we see, everything we touch, everything we do. That is what our world is made of. Your world will mirror you. Once we unlearn that fight and learn the love, we see the love within and around us, and our worlds become love. Your world and your life mirror what is going on inside of you. Fighting against ourselves is a huge mistake, even when we use it as motivation.

"You are your competition." or "It is you vs. you."

This is damaging and harmful thinking, fueling the fight in our minds. We don't have to fight against ourselves. We don't have to fight against anything. We are here to love. After all, love is all that we are at the soul level.

The truth is this, you are *your masterpiece,* and it is you with you...loving you. Once you realize this, the relationship with yourself can heal. Love yourself, and love will become you. You will see yourself as the art that you are.

Unlearn your need to compete. Competing against others steals from your focus on your journey and competing against yourself keeps you focusing on the fight inside. Unlearning the fight inside is vital to being in the moment. If you stay where you are or bring yourself back to where you are when your mind wanders, there is no need for a fight anymore. Stopping allows you to be in the moment and being in the moment makes it easier to stop the fight. Once you learn this, the cycle of fighting against the future or past becomes a beautiful process of loving the moment you are in. What you are fighting against can never be the Now. It is something in your past or something in your future. Be here. Be the Now.

Unlearn trying to "fix" the past or make up for the past. The past version of you is no longer you. Work the stories stuck because as long as they are stuck in the past, so are you. Once you have worked on those stories, let them go. Relax into the now, knowing that every second of your history is why you are here now—every second needed to happen to create this version of you. To bring you to love, to get you to joy, and to bring you here.

Let go of trying to control the future. Having goals is amazing, and we want to unlearn our attachment to those goals. What happens if those goals don't happen?

What happens if you choose a different path instead? What happens if something out of your control chooses a different path for you? Did you fail?

No

You learned the correct path and are now on the proper new track. There are no mistakes. Where you are is where you are supposed to be. What you are doing is what you are supposed to be doing. What you are feeling is what you are supposed to be feeling.

We are taught to push ourselves aside to get to the next step, we are taught that showing emotions is a sign of weakness, and we are taught that we can silence ourselves with external resources.

Unlearn your need to distract. With food, liquor, reality TV, or sports. Do these things help you grow? Do they make you better? I am not saying that you can't entertain yourself but recognize if you are using any of these things as a distraction.

Does a challenging conversation at work have you running for a glass of wine at 5 pm? Does an emotional break-up have you running for chocolate ice cream by the pint? Does a stressful day have you binge-watching a TV show that you don't even like? Does your need to be accepted by your parents or a spouse have you attaching your worth to something outside of yourself, like whether a sports team with no idea you exist wins or loses?

These distractions all have one thing in common. They are designed to take you out of the moment. We turn to them to turn off our feelings.

Staying in the moment requires feeling. Any feeling felt all the way through is beautiful, and I promise you that the feeling will become more natural as you begin to feel.

You won't want to shut off the stress after the conversation with your boss, the sadness of a breakup, or even being misunderstood by those closest to you. You will realize that you love yourself, honor your feelings, and know they are there for a reason. Sit still, breathe, relax, and let the feeling be with you. We were meant to feel, and being able to feel all the way through is a gift and a beautiful part of this human experience. You will learn that you can grow through any experience, and when you allow what is there to be there instead of running for a temporary vice, you truly expand.

Unlearn the lie that you have one "right way", and your soul has one purpose on earth. There are many paths for you. You can walk many paths, and they are all exactly where you need to be. Unlearn that not achieving what you set out to diminishes any worth. Remember that you can't reduce your value because you were born with it.

Unlearn the lies that keep you in one box for your whole life, and keep you focused on one destination.

Unlearn the words that keep you small; they are not valid. If you live for one purpose or goal at a time, you will be blinded to all the moments along the way, and you can miss how much beauty there is. The most beauty is in the moments, way more than the few prominent destinations we see, and you will still get those if you focus on the moment. They will become part of it, a by-product.

Once you unlearn, you leave room to start the relearning processes. We must first shed the parts of us that are not us, the stuff we picked up along the way. Whether it was something we taught ourselves for protection or something we were taught was the right way, we can let it go now, and we can be who we are. Unlearn the distraction, unlearn the need to shut feelings out, and unlearn your patterns. Honor every part of your human experience. Honor all that you feel and love all that you are, right here, right now, at this moment that you are in.

Chapter 5:

Nourish

Nourishment goes way beyond food.
How do you take care of your mood?

Do listen to the experts you see on your scroll?
Or do you trust that you already know?

Know your body, know what it needs?
Listen to what it wants, hear what it heeds?

Health and nourishment are innate in you.
Trust me, you know what to do.

So, take a deep breath and listen down deep.
What do you want to toss away, what do you keep?

And learn this about food, it is art.
You know what to create deep in your heart.

Treat yourself like someone you deeply love.
It is needed to put yourself above.

So, start looking at nourishment in a new way.
Minute by minute, day by day

When you think of the word nourish, is food the first thing that comes to mind? It is for me, so if so, we are in the same boat.

So much more goes into nourishing food, and it can be so much less rigid in nourishing your body.

Sunlight nourishes your body, stretching nourishes your body, and sleep nourishes your body. Nourishing your body is doing what feels authentic to you. That is how I started looking at it; my body and I have become much friendlier.

Do you feel balanced and connected when you are out in nature? Then nature nourishes your body. Do you feel aligned when you are around other people? Then you are nourished by those connections. Do you feel like you get a recharge when you spend time alone? Then you are feeding yourself with your solitude? When you listen to yourself, you will hear what you want. Following that voice (or intuition) is what takes practice. Nourishment is deeply personal, and it is different for everyone. Your nutrition may look different than mine did and does, and that is ok. I am sharing my personal story here as a guide, an example of how I started trusting myself fully.

Speaking of my personal experience, I didn't know what nourishment meant for a long time.

I am very grateful to Kim for teaching me most of the ideas and topics in this chapter. Her teachings truthfully changed the game for me regarding nourishing my body. Earlier, I dove into my stories of the past and how my toxic relationship with my body and nourishment started. I thought that healthy meant skinny, so nourishing myself was eating next to nothing at times.

In other words, I was depleting myself and telling myself I was nourishing myself. Other times I lived on chicken, spinach, and sweet potatoes and ate that for lunch and dinner daily even if I didn't want them. I was not listening to myself and choked down the same meal daily because I thought that was what I had to do to be nourished [skinny]. I have learned that proper nourishment will not feel like something I *must do*.

I would count every macro, every calorie. I remember one "diet" I was on that said I shouldn't chew gum because it throws off your breathing and causes you to bring in more oxygen which can cause bloating. I am all for breath and breathing control, and that was way too restrictive for me. Most of my diets were so restrictive that I couldn't maintain them.

I tried all the major "fad diets." I will not call anyone out, but if you can name it, I likely tried it. I downloaded countless "weight loss apps." The number of health food shakes that I gagged down makes me sad inside. I would track everything that I put into my body to the point where it was no longer sustainable, and I would "fall off" and want to binge. Restrictive eating is not nourishment.

Nourishment is knowing and trusting your body and that it knows what it wants and what it needs. When you are in alignment with yourself, nutrition becomes effortless. Restricting myself to the point where I could no longer sustain it. Leading to another fall off and a period of binging all the foods I had cut out.

Insert guilt and shame of yet another failed diet, usually followed by emotional eating and drinking after high school; that is where the hidden bag of chocolates would come in. In college, that is where the Smirnoff flavored vodka and keg beer would come in, not to mention sweets from the dining hall, not to mention all the pizza places that stayed open until 4 am in that town. After college, that is where the bottle of red wine or the six-pack (or 12-pack) of Modelos would come in, coupled with whatever third-party food delivery service I ordered and ate on autopilot.

Add in barely touching nature and spending most of my days in the classrooms, the basement bedroom of my apartment, and then crowded bars that mainly smelled like mold and stale beer. So, I was spending my time in environments that did not foster connection, eating and drinking substances that enabled the opposite of any semblance of self-connection. I had no awareness of what I was doing to myself. Then after college, I continued the cycle for another six years, bouncing from growingly depleting jobs and jumping between one-bedroom apartments.

I am not telling you not to track macros. I am not telling you all diets are doomed to fail, and if you have found something that works for you and brings you joy in your life, do that. It is incredible how different we all are; some things feel nourishing to one person and feel like a gut bomb to another.

If you authentically decide for yourself and do not ignore your body's queues, I am all for whatever system works for you. Make sure you are holding love for yourself, though, because without that, nothing is sustainable.

Remember, I am stating my experience with yoyo dieting and restrictive eating. I know many people, specifically women, that connected food and exercise with being tools to make you skinny or other vices that made you overweight, and nothing else. There is so much more joy in nourishment than that. Food is not a tool to make you skinny. Food is fuel, and when you enjoy it, you will be free from the restraints you have felt.

I was also eating or drinking to calm the sadness of failed diets. As discussed, it got to the point that I had gotten so used to being able to numb my emotions that I didn't even realize I was shutting them all off. Eating and drinking seemed to soothe me until they didn't. Comfort food and alcohol would hit the same, causing me a few minutes of pleasure and then almost immediately feeling like garbage and then going back for more to soothe that discomfort.

Allow the discomfort to be there if you eat something that causes it. No judgment, no guilt, and no shame necessary. Recognize how you feel, and then move on. This is how we grow awareness, and this is how we learn to eat to support the person we want to be and the way we want to feel.

Nourishment is food-related, as we have outlined thus far, and nutrition also allows you to feel your emotions all the way through. Once you learn that emotions are beautiful and necessary to your human experience, you unknowingly permit yourself to stop running for all the vices you put in place to shut them off.

Food is related to feeling. The feeling is nourishing. Crying out what we want to cry out is healthy. Laughing so hard our stomach hurts is medicine. Feeling gloomy is as good for our soul as feeling cheerful is.

Feeling your emotions is the first step to fully and completely nourishing your body. Feeling your feelings allows you to look inside, listen, and choose what you authentically want to consume without unresolved emotions blocking the way and steering the ship.

Feel, let it pass, and then make the decision. Freely.

Also, get down on some sweets now and again. Drink hot chocolate during Christmas time. Eat the appetizer when you dine with your friends *IF YOU WANT TO*. That is the key.

You don't have to eat foods you don't want because they are there, don't just eat them because your friends pressure you. I promise that after a few "no, I am good's" they will stop pressuring you. Say it confidently, and when you decide you want the food, eat it with confidence. Making decisions for your true self is something to celebrate. Every time you do that, do it with pride for yourself.

I also promise you this, the delivery of your yeses and no's will create the reaction that your friends and family give. If you meekly say no, they will think you want it and assure you it is ok. Be loud about the way you feel and trust yourself fully.

Being out to dinner with my friends and family, and they offer the fried cheesy appetizer to me, and I honestly do not want it because I have learned that fried and cheese = Kaitlynn feeling like garbage.

In the beginning, I would have said something along the lines of:

"Oh no, I can't eat that," and I would have delivered it non-confidently and wondered what they would think of me. I was scared that they would judge me if I didn't eat it, scared that I would be judged if I did.

I tended to overthink everything I ate. Whereas if people were pressuring me, I would think to myself. "Oh man, I can't eat that. This person will judge me for eating it because they know I am trying to eat healthily, and that goes along with everything I say I am," or "Oh, they are going to think I am too good for the appetizer that is not going to promote the things I want to feel or the person I want to be, so I better take one."

I would base MY decision on what I ate on what other people thought. It does not get more inauthentic to me than that. And you cannot authentically nourish yourself if you are not authentic to yourself in the first place. If you want to take control of your life and body, learn what you want, listen inside, and then say and do what you want out loud.

Most people will respect your no's regardless of how you say them. Some people will not, and they will want to reassure you that you can stray away from your focus or that they can help you make decisions for your happiness.

Here are some ways to say no to the people who think they know you better than you know yourself.

"No"

"No, thank you."

"Nope, I'm good."

"No, I am excited about my dinner."

"No, you enjoy it!"

And they may push back and pressure you once and then use one of those responses, and it will be done. After being firm in your no's a few times, people will stop asking.

Sometimes I eat the appetizer because sometimes I want it. I am more likely to make my decisions for myself because I have started truly listening to myself.

A great affirmation that has changed my nourishment game is:

"I make my decisions with love for myself," and yes, this affirmation can go far beyond decisions in nourishment, and it is super helpful in this case.

When you think about what you want, how you want to feel, and what you wish to do now, you can always make the decision most aligned with you. Sometimes that may be listening to your taste buds or hormones, and most of the time, if you take a breath and listen, you will decide what best supports the person you want to become and how you want to feel. You will choose to keep the moment you want to have.

Also, I have started looking at food as art (Thanks, Kim!). Food is so beautiful, and creating it is magic. This makes cooking fun and my dishes colorful.

The brightness of the vegetables and fruits makes my plates much more fun. Food is a beautiful way to tap into my creative side, and what better art to create than what I am about to fuel my body with?

When you cook your food, you prepare your body to eat. Digestion starts when cooking, so if you skip that part and order food more than you are cooking it, the body misses the beginning of digestion. I love cooking my food. I cook to create instead of cooking to eat.

Also, a side effect of tapping into my creative energy when cooking is dancing and singing in the kitchen while I am creating the dishes. I went from slapping food together, boring, mundane, and low vibe, and cooking the food to have something to eat, not being in the moment, to cooking the food to cook the food, and to having a party with myself in the kitchen while I cook.

Another side effect. The food is even more delicious, not because I am trying to make it delicious, but because I am looking at it as art and enjoying the creative process of it. I put my time into it. I put spices and flavors into it. Each meal is a masterpiece.

Breakfast is my favorite to create, sweet potato skillets, avocado toast, and egg sandwiches. There is so much color. Plus, starting the morning off on such a cheerful and nourishing note is amazing.

Nourishing can be for the body, mind, soul, and spirit. All food nourishes. Please read that again and learn all food nourishes. The choices that you make come down to having an awareness of how food makes you feel.

And once you notice how the food you're eating is affecting you physically and mentally, you will make much more authentic choices to you in the time that you are making them. You will be aware that certain foods make you feel bloated or sleepy. So if you know what is causing the sluggish feeling, you will choose to go for something that does not cause you to feel that way.

Or

You will make a choice knowing that while you may not be energized after the meal, you may feel bloated or sluggish, and you are choosing with that awareness in mind.

Both choices are ok, and being in tune with your body will likely make you make the former choice more often.

Another thing I have started to do when selecting my meals is, instead of asking myself, "What do I want to eat?" I ask myself, "What do I want to feel like?"

Sometimes my taste buds run the show and make the call. For most meals, most snacks, and most days, I make the decision that best supports my mental clarity, focus, and energy.

I have reconnected with my intuition, which allows me to eat authentically and intuitively.

You will know what will nourish you, and when you become aligned and balanced in yourself, you can feel what you want and what is suitable for you. And whether that is a nature walk or a bar of chocolate, the feeling around it will become neutral. Any choice you make will be made consciously and feel equally good.

Want to know what else nourishes, balances, and reconnects you just as much, if not more than food? Your breath.

Chapter 6:
Breathe

You want to see the beauty
Focus on the way you breathe
Keep your breath slow
and watch the stress leave

Breath keeps us calm
Breath gives a life
Breath stops the fight
Breath stops the strife

Breathe through your story
Breathe through your day
Breathe and look forward
Let your breath guide the way

Want to slow time
Breathe in and breathe deep.
In the moment your in
yourself you will keep

Breathing seems so apparent. We are constantly breathing. We are taught in school that breathing is involuntary, and we don't even have to think about it. This is true but walking around with unconscious breathing is a fast way to rip yourself from the moment and put yourself into a stressed state. We want to breathe intentionally. It will change your world.

Where is your breath right now? In your chest? Many people breathe shallowly to their chests. That is stress breathing. We want to be breathing deep into our bellies.

Before you continue, just stop.

Breathe in slowly, counting - 1.2.3.4

Exhale and count - 1.2.3.4.5.6.7.8

Now repeat that three more times.

How is that? Better, right?

One of the quickest ways to take yourself out of the moment is to lose control of your breath, and most people need to learn how crucial intentional breathing is. Many people are moving through life, have their breath trapped in their chests, and are constantly stressed. It is difficult to help someone when they are in that state and difficult to help yourself when you are in that state.

If you want better control of your life, take back control of your breath, focus on staying low and slow, and send every breath down into your belly. You can take command of most situations by sending your breath into your root. While it may not change the external moments around you, it will immediately calm your nervous system, and your ability to be in the moment and make decisions will belong to you again.

Human babies naturally breathe in their bellies, and then somewhere along the way, that can change and usually does. As we develop stress and learn responsibilities, we can easily forget to take the time to breathe. Ironic because breathing deeply is the antidote for so much of our stress and anxiety. Breathing low and slowly is the way to stay in the moment, making time pass slower. Do you want to remain present at this moment? Master breath control because you will be fighting an uphill battle without it. And remember, we want to unlearn the fight.

Breathing low and slow, like most other topics in this book, is a practice at first. It is something that will take a concentration in the beginning. A great way to start training yourself to *breeeeaaatthhheee* is with meditation.

To begin practicing meditation, starting with 10 minutes a day in the mornings is a game changer. Remember, starting may feel unnatural, just like anything you are new at. You are allowed to be new. It is allowed to feel bizarre or out of place. You are entitled to want to get up and move, and you can overthink through meditation. You can let whatever is there; if you focus on breathing slowly, you do everything correctly. I promise.

Meditating to slow your breathing will set you on the path to keeping your belly breathing through the day. The more you practice and the longer you practice, the more effortless it will become. Think of it as any other skill you have learned in life. Remember that it is an important skill, too, as your breathing can affect how you see the world around you.

Breathing shallowly is exhausting. We are tiring ourselves out just by breathing when we breathe fast and in our chest. Regulating our breathing regulates our energy and our nervous system. We can keep ourselves much more balanced through intentional breathing. Also, keeping ourselves calm in stressful situations that usually cause us to be highly anxious allows us the time and clarity to look at our situation thoroughly. Breath is one of the best ways to put yourself back in the moment you are in very quickly.

Take another deep breath now.

Inhale - 1.2.3.4

Exhale -2.3.4.5.6.7.8

Repeat it three times.

Day to Day breath control is key and a baseline to keeping yourself balanced, even, and in this moment. We can take our breathing practice even deeper by incorporating breathwork into our lives.

Breathwork

Breathwork connects us, mind, body, and soul. Mind, body, and soul connections are essential in staying in this moment; breathwork can be a significant key in connecting those three. There are many different types and styles of breathwork, and they come in varying intensity levels. Any breathwork that I have done has helped me learn to stop fighting and start loving.

Breathwork has many physical benefits; some include reduced blood pressure, reduced inflammation and pain relief, improved energy and immunity, improved digestion, and helps detoxifying the body. When our bodies feel good, keeping ourselves where we are is much easier than worrying about the future.

The benefits of breathwork reach beyond the physical and support deeper into our mental and spiritual well-being. Breathwork cultivates stillness and openness and allows us to be in our state of love. It gives us the freedom to explore the moment and our space truly. Breathwork can also help us supercharge affirmations, release trauma, or release physical or mental blocks within us.

Breathwork takes us into ourselves and allows us to connect with the true us fully. We can tap into our creative sides when we take the time to look inside us. Anytime I write, it is after breathwork because it allows me to reconnect myself and bring my most authentic me to these pages.

I meditate, I move my body, and then I do breathwork, and then I sit, and I write. It is the same with coloring or drawing. I see myself in my creations after I take the time to sit down and connect myself to mind, body, and soul.

Connection of mind, body, and soul is imperative to authenticity, as they are imperative to being right here, right where you are. Meditation, working out, coloring, writing, and music - are activities that help activate one or two of the three.

Breathwork hits all three. Breathwork connects your mind, body, and soul all on its own. All of the activities mentioned above are powerful on their own. Breathwork connects you to you and to all that is. You can tap into your full potential because you are reaching your entire self and remembering all that you will ever need or have already lives within you.

Breathing is vital as it gives us life. We can use our breath to stay precisely where we are. Breathing slowly and deeply can change our lives from stressful to blissful. Keeping yourself downregulated with your breath is the best way to balance your central nervous system.

Breathing slowly can also be combined with your words to supercharge the words. Inserting breath after a powerful statement sends that statement deep into your core and your root. Supercharging your words with breath can profoundly impact your ability to do what you say. You will do and be who you want to be.

Try our exercise this way:

Say out loud, "I am right here."

Inhale - 1.2.3.4

Exhale - 1.2.3.4.5.6.7.8

Say that out loud with the breath three times.

Now pay attention to how that feels. In your mind? In your body? In your soul? Breath combined with words can change your entire mindset and your entire life.

Breath can help us with our relationships with ourselves and our relationship with others; when we are breathing low and slow, we allow others to regulate their nervous system. Also, keeping our mind and body, and soul connected can help us with difficult conversations. We can change the entire dynamic of a discussion by just controlling our breath.

Breath creates awareness, time, clarity, and space, which can also impact our decision-making. We are likely to react authentically if we have our breath under control.

Breathing well helps us to listen to ourselves. When we slow our breath down, we concentrate on the simplest thing we can do. Simplifying your world returns you to the moment. You are connected to the *Now* when you focus on each breath moving in and out of your body.

Chapter 7:
Move

Can you listen?
Stop and hear
When and how to move
Yourself you can steer

Stop and take a second
Hear your body speak
It will tell you your strengths
And what does it seek

Your body will guide you
And tell you how to move
You will learn what to do
You will find your groove

Is it getting up early
And walking outside?
Is it stretching and finding
The spots that would hide?

Do you want to lift heavy
And build up your strength
Movement is yours

To do your own way

Start to listen
And you will hear
What your body wants
It will be clear.

Then there is movement...

Did I mention that's something I got to heal too? I probably have indirectly, and here is the story behind that side of my journey. Forcing yourself to move in a way that feels terrible is unsustainable. Especially if you are doing it to move a number on a scale or to drop a pants size, that is living for the future. When you stop, breathe, and listen, your body will tell you what to move and how. Your body will tell you what you want and what would help it at that moment. Your health will become effortless and authentic.

I told you all that I got my first gym membership at 13. I don't know how old I was, younger than I can remember when I learned that skinny equals a higher worth. I had this conditioning that I chased for close to 20 years. My weight fluctuated (it still does), up and down. As people commented on how "good I looked" when I was thinner, my perceived worth would skyrocket. When the number on the scale moved up, and the compliments dwindled, my perceived value plummeted.

It was all a lie, though.

First, worth is not based on any part of your physical appearance or health. It is not "based" on anything. My value is my value, infinite, and has been since the day I was born. So is yours.

So reread these words and let them sink in right here and now.

Your worth is already within you. You were *born* worthy.

Nothing you do can make you worthless, and nothing you can do can make you worth more. Your worth is expansive and ever-reaching; all you have to do is know that and hold that in your heart.

You do not have to do one workout for your entire life, and your worth is as high as someone who goes to the gym consistently for their whole life. That was such a struggle for me to learn. I couldn't understand that. I thought I had to be pretty and skinny, among other personality traits, to be worth anything to anyone. The movement became about working my food off, pushing myself *way* past my limit.

Lastly, your worth does not depend on anyone else. Not a parent, not a friend, not a partner, not a sibling, not a child. *NO ONE.* They also do not get to determine your worth. If you are alive, you are worth everything.

So, back to 13-year-old Kaitlynn. The celebrities I looked up to were skinny and blonde, so I wanted to be like them. I had super blonde hair that started darkening as I got older, so I added highlights.

I got my gym membership, and I remember using the Stairmaster, then going straight to the treadmill and the elliptical. All cardio, I didn't care about being strong. Make me skinny. I will drag myself here exhausted. I will come twice a day. I will restrict calories and work out. That is how I will maintain my childlike body, not realizing that I was healthy and beautiful the way I was growing. And all that I was doing was building years of distrust with my body.

That was the beginning of the extreme restriction and rigorous workouts that would lead to a fall, usually accompanied by a binge. I was never listening to my body. Maybe not ever, but very rarely. I didn't care what I wanted to do. I was either doing what I "had" to do and dragging myself somewhere I didn't want to be or self-soothing with a period where I would sleep and lay around, barely moving. There was no middle ground and no balance or consistency at that time.

In fact, instead of listening to myself, I was forcing my body to listen to me. I created a divide, a distrust between myself and my body. We became so separate even though we were living as one. I would spend years in this cycle, deepening and deepening this cycle of distrust that only now have I begun to be able to heal. And it is a process; after so much yo-yo-ing, I am finally telling my body it is ok. She is safe and allowed to be whatever she needs to be to feel safe with me. I still have goals for myself, and now instead of losing the most weight possible in the shortest amount of time possible, my dreams look like this.

• Listen to my body and prove to her that she can trust me again

• Move the way I authentically want to (this includes a ton of nature walks and 20–30-minute workouts most days)

• Meditate and breathe to keep stress hormones down

• Affirm in the mirror that I am beautiful and safe and love myself the way I am every morning.

I love my body now, the way she is. She has supported me through, quite literally, everything that has gone on in my life. She has been here with me the whole time; even as I said horrible things to her, she kept going, kept pushing to get me here, to a place where we are friends, and now and only now can we have a healthy relationship with movement. My body supports me. She takes care of me. She always has.

Here is a spell I wrote (again, in coaching with Kim)

My body always takes care of me, regardless of the decisions I make.

My body is always moving.

My body is always sitting still.
My body always carries me through life.

My body always forgives me.

I support my body in all ways by connecting myself.

I support my body in all ways.

Regarding movement and body image, it goes back to a common theme in this book.

Stop fighting! Start loving!

Fall in love with moving your body; it feels good, and she is proud to show you what she can do. Fall in love with moving your body because your body has always loved moving you. Find a way to move that feels like love.

For me, that is walks; walks are magical. Walking in nature is my favorite type of movement and feels good at almost every stage and cycle of my life. If you want to do something amazing for your body while clearing your head, regulating your nervous system, and slowing your breath down, then go out and take a walk.

We are nature, and moving in nature is the most realigning thing we can do for ourselves.

Breathe when you move to connect yourself even more profoundly. Before you proceed, take a deep breath to settle in and then start to move in a way that feels good to you.

Sit back, close your eyes, and take a big deep breath. Did you think you were getting away without any other deep breaths in the book? Because there are more to come, I promise.

Breathe when you move to connect yourself even more profoundly. Breathe before you move. Make sure to take a deep breath to settle in.

Start by scanning your body. Are there places that have sensations? Any pain, discomfort, or tension? Would it feel good to stretch anywhere in your body? Go ahead and take a second to start stretching if you want to.

Stretching, like walking, is another one of my favorites and is a gateway to all other movements. Stretching is looking into ourselves and noticing what is there and then addressing it, paying attention to it, and caring for it.

So, once I breathe deeply, scan my body for potential spots of awareness, and stretch, I am in touch with my body.

What wants to move? Do I want to reach for my dumbbells, or do I want to hop on my rower? Do I want to grab my resistance bands? Do I want to go for an hour-long walk? What would feel authentic to me right now and help my body feel amazing too?

Then I started to move and realized how beautiful movement can be when fully connected to my body, mind, and spirit.

Movement doesn't have to be daunting. It can be soft, and it can be light. It can be whatever would work for you and connects you to the moment.

Movement and Food

Movement and food were shared with me as this connected thing for so long, and I get it. It is a calorie in/calorie out ideology, and for a long time, that is how many people were taught about food and exercise. Movement and food should be considered separate ways to connect with yourself.

"You must move to "burn off" what you eat. You must move to burn more calories than you eat. If you eat dessert, make sure you go for a walk when you get home to balance it out." These are some "lessons" I picked up along the way.

At an elementary level, the above statements make sense to many people, and they were how I lived for so long until I looked inside and started listening to myself. On a "not so simple level," those statements are garbage advice, or at least, were for me. Working out or moving is not a punishment for eating. Movement is a beautiful connection with yourself.

Remembering eating is nourishment and is not a punishable offense.

Trust yourself.

Now is the time to disconnect food and movement.

What feels good to eat? How do I want to move?

These questions *do not* have to depend on each other. You do not have to go for a 2-mile run after eating a big dinner. Stop *punishing your body* for fueling it.

It all comes down to trusting yourself. Trust your decisions, what you do, and who you are. You know yourself better than anyone else, and you can make decisions without rigid restrictions when you are connected with yourself. When you are willing to listen and act on what you hear, alignment happens, and making these decisions is natural.

Exercise and movement are beautiful when we stop and think about what we want to do. Where are we feeling strong that day? Where can we work more? Do I want to shift my focus to somewhere different in my body, or do I want to do something I know I do well? It can be looked at in such feminine energy, creative way.
Movement can be looked at as art, just as food can. Your days are masterpieces, and what you do now creates those masterpieces.

Don't expect to feel the same way every day. Don't expect to feel the same strength every day. That goes for everyone, especially if you are a woman. We go through cycles every month. We will feel different at different times of the month, weeks, and sometimes days. If you are highly sensitive, you may feel different from minute to minute (I am looking at myself here).

So, take a second to listen to yourself. What would feel good to move?

Stop forcing yourself to do things that hurt and feel diminishing just because "that is what you did last week, and it felt great," and especially stop doing something because someone on social media told you it would "flatten your tummy in 10 days". Human bodies are all different, and while we are effortlessly connected to everyone because we are all that is, our bodies work differently. Move in a way that soothes your body and feels good to your soul. Work with yourself instead of against yourself. You already know what to do. It is already inside of you.

Staying present in each moment you are in can lead to beautiful experiences with moving your body, and beautiful authentic experiences with moving your body can help you stay current at the moment you are in. Movement and the moment are in a symbiotic relationship. They both support each other because they support your connection to yourself.

Chapter 8:
Words

The words you keep out and the words you keep in
Determine whether you lose or you win

Let your words be your story, your words be your guide
And inside your head, don't let your words hide

Inside your head your words start to swirl
And into a tornado they can whirl

See words can be the most beautiful tool
Or a weapon, and turn you into a fool

Use your words to create your magic
Instead of writing something more tragic

Words will shape what becomes real
Can give you the world, or they can steal

So be careful when deciding the words you choose
Your reality is created by the ones you use

Oh, words. Lovely, beautiful, magical words. I adore words. Words are magic, and awareness of them has been one of the fundamental shifts in my life. Words are important because when we speak, we create our realities, shaping our worlds and putting those words into the universe. You can create, and words can be used as a tool, or they can be used against you; you get to decide.

Shout out to the Enlifted Coaching Community, where all my coaches have come from, and I have also been certified. There is no better method than storywork, which is the method taught by Enlifted, when it comes to teaching about words and how to make our language work for us instead of against us. Mark England was the first to teach me about the words I was using and help me see how much power they held and how much magic they had in them.

I was giving my power away with the words I used to use. Turning what could have been my driving forces into the things that blocked me. When I started learning how to translate my sentences, my entire world started changing. I knew that our lives are made up of stories. The stories are made up of words. And the words we choose dictate our reality. What reality do you want to create? Change your words, and you can and will change your life.

Do you remember how I talked to myself from my story? I used words and language against myself. I was using my words as weapons instead of magic wands. The words I was saying were too horrible to say out loud. My toxic relationship with myself was mostly hidden. Some people had an idea of the hateful things I said to myself, mainly that war was only mine and something I was trying to fight alone. I had worked with a talk therapist before this, and her intentions were great, and while therapy would help for a short time after the session, the pressure would start to build again soon after. When I began coaching with Mark, he showed me how to go back into the story, look at it, dissect it and change the words in a way that still rang true and empowered me instead of causing me to crumble and fall.

Remember, we are unlearning the fight and learning to embody our love. Words are a great place to continue and solidify in this process. Once you learn to breathe in your belly and control that breath to work for you, you can start switching up your language because, as I mentioned, you can use that breath to supercharge your new words and help them stick in your core. It is wise to get your breath in control first or simultaneously because an aligned and balanced nervous system will help when recreating your stories. This is how you create your core values and learn the true you.

There are a few different components within language. Different ways our words can work, ways they can hold power, and other ways they can take away control.

Do you pressure yourself to do certain activities, implying a sense of shame or guilt if you do not get those tasks done? Do you turn activities that you could enjoy or make you feel amazing at this moment into activities that are chores?

Check out these examples:

"I should go to the gym today."

"I have to cook dinner for my kids tonight."

Both sentences make the task sound like a task. They are also pressuring you to go somewhere in the future. There are simple changes that take the pressure of language and those feelings of guilting yourself out of these sentences.

"I will go to the gym tonight."

"I get to cook dinner for my kids tonight."

In the second example, the drama is removed from the sentences. The feeling of "not wanting to do" those tasks is removed.

I once had someone tell me how much she loves cooking for her son, and she told me that cooking for her family was her love language. Then she told me she "had to cook" for her family a few sentences later. When we switched from "have to" to "get to," her body immediately relaxed. She smiled and said, "yes, that is true. I get to."

This is a simple example of a simple switch that can change how you look at your life. By realizing how much you love doing what you do, those daily moments become a joyful activity instead of a busy task.

You can also supercharge these statements by adding a because at the end.

"I will go to the gym today because I love how I feel after and love taking care of myself."

"I will cook dinner for my son because I enjoy showing my love through cooking."

These are solid sentences that, even though they may be future thoughts, are simple and to the point. Pressuring yourself can cause you to dwell on the future casting even longer. When you flip the words and take the drama out, you are letting the thought be and putting yourself right back in the moment you are in.

Do you use softening words in your language? In the Enlifted world, we call these soft talk keywords. Some examples are, hope, perhaps, and probably; take a second to think about why you would use those words. What would be the purpose of them in your language? Something that I hear a lot is that those words seem more polite and less intense.

There is, of course, time for these words. However, they can often be omitted to make our speaking more transparent, concise, and easier to understand.

If you reduce your soft talk words by half what you use now, you will feel like a different person. That is how it was taught to me, and it has become true.

Take this example:

I am thinking I might go to the gym today vs. I am going to the gym today.

The first sentence explains why we won't go to the gym - "thinking" and "might."

The second sentence is solid, and the chances of us doing what we say we will do go up with omitting those two words.

A great place to start practicing removing your soft talk words is in emails and text messages because you can type and edit. I challenge you to begin eliminating soft talk today and see if you feel more empowered and clearer in what you say.

Make your words solid. That will also help you stay in the moment because it provides more clarity and less space to become fuzzy minded. Clarity is a large part of staying in the moment you are in. Use precise words and see the moment too.

A great way that I learned to bring awareness to your soft talk is a 7-day soft talk challenge. This is straight from the Enlifted method, and it is incredible. I have done many 7-day soft talk challenges myself. Go ahead and grab a sheet of paper and write the words down on it:

Maybe
Might
Perhaps
Possibly
Think
Hopefully
One day
Suppose
Almost like
Guess
Try

Sort of
Kind of

Go stick that piece of paper on your bathroom mirror (or somewhere else where you will see it daily).

This will help you see them more clearly and reduce the use of these words effortlessly.

We also want to ensure our words empower us because words are powerful regardless. We get to choose if they are empowering or disempowering. What will help us live more in our moment and as the people we want to be? Giving ourselves excuses by using ambiguous words is one of the easiest ways to avoid accountability for ourselves, and our presence and awareness depend on us taking responsibility for our lives.

Another way we can easily pass accountability and responsibility from ourselves is by using projections. When we project, we seek to blame others for our shortcomings or for the things we are blocked from in our lives.
"They don't respect me."

"They never listen."

"He ruined my life."

While these projections may hold some accuracy, saying and living by these statements spells them into becoming your reality, so let's take the last one. Let's take our power back.

"He ruined my life."

Does that person hold all that power? Is that entirely accurate? Is your life ruined? Is there anything you can do to continue moving forward? Focusing on your ruined life, you will continue looking at your shattered life. Your life will stay "ruined."

A great way to look at projections differently is to change them into an "I" statement. This process may sting at first, and if you trust the process all the way through, you will soon feel empowered.

"I ruined my life."
Accurate? No

So, what can you do? How can you take your power back?

"I am rebuilding my life."

Which can further translate in the following ways:

"I rebuild my life," or "I rebuilt my life," or "I build my life."

See? It stings at first, and then it is very empowering. Let it sting, feel the sting, and move with it. Once you have thought it all through, you can move to the beauty. You can move into a life you own.

What you focus on, you will get; what you say to yourself, you will be. Remember, we want to keep our vision of what we do want, what we can do, and what will drive us toward being that person. What can we do now to be the person we want to be?

Ready for my favorite type of language? Affirmations!! Speaking in the affirmative has allowed me to transform my life completely. Changing statements with negations into affirmation statements has allowed me to see everything possible in my life and realize all the beauty there.

Think about when you tell yourself you can't do something, and you stop the possibility of ever doing it. When you say that you can do it or learn to do it, you open all the doors for yourself. Your world expands the moment you flip negations to affirmations.

Writing our affirmations down is a fantastic way to supercharge them. A word written down is solid and will feel like it is written in stone. So, do you want to live with more presence? If you read this book, the answer to that question is a yes.

Do you have a sticky note, a note card, or a piece of paper handy? If so, grab one and a pen; if it is not sticky, grab some scotch tape too.

Say these statements out loud with a breath in between each one because your deep breaths will push the affirmation down into your core.

"I am present." BREATHE

"I am aware." BREATHE

"I am right here." BREATHE

"I am at this moment." BREATHE

Do any of those feel more emotionally charged than the others? Write that one down on your paper. If there is more than one, write them all down. Stick that piece of paper next to your soft talk challenge. Repeat these affirmations daily.

Remember what I said about talking to yourself as if you are already the person you want to become? These affirmation statements will train your brain and body to be more in the moment by simply stating them.

A spell is a word or sequence of words believed to hold magical power. Is there anything more magical than a sequence of words that takes you from living in the past or future and drops you right into the moment you are in?

Our words are spells. What kind of magic are you casting for yourself? Is it dark magic that keeps you in the war in your mind, with haunting stories of the past or terrifying thoughts of the future, or is it light magic that frees you to see all the light and all the beauty around you? Is it the type of magic that allows you to live for all the moments you are in? To be happy and love in any emotion that you're feeling.

Do your words even allow your feelings to come forward? Do you let yourself cry and emote? Or are you stifling your feelings because you were taught they were a sign of weakness? Feelings are strengths, not weaknesses.

You are allowed to feel. Tell yourself that.

"I am allowed to feel." BREATHE

Add it to your affirmations list on your bathroom mirror if that makes sense. Trust me; I realize that adding affirmations to and talking to yourself in the mirror can feel unnatural at first. After a while, the words will feel easy to say, and the affirmations will be words you believe. And once you accept the words, you have created the person that embodies the words. You get to live as that person.

Your affirmations are an excellent example of an action you can take right now to start moving toward your goals and shifting into the expanded version of who you want to be.

The list of affirmations is expansive and infinite, and the reasons you choose certain ones over others are up to you. Say these affirmations out loud. Do they feel powerful? Do they feel like a magical spell? Those are the ones you should incorporate into your daily practice. Here are a few simple, powerful affirmations that can help you start incorporating this practice into your life today.

"I am enough."
"I am strong."
"I am love."
"I am joy."
"I am brilliant."
"I am mine."
"I am consistent."
"I am happy."
"I am allowing."
"I create me."

Speaking in affirmations changed the course of my life, and I have watched them do the same for countless others. If you are open to change, it will happen.

Affirmations will help you to look at the world differently. They will train you to start looking for what is beautiful and unique. Instead of looking at what you can't do and focusing on that, you will begin to see all the possibilities available. You will realize that you already have the power inside of you to learn any skill you desire to learn.

Remember that words are magical. Treat them as such. They can light up your whole world or start a war within you. Use them for love; use their power for good. Inside your head, you say a lot; you hear a lot. Let those words work for you. Talk to yourself like a friend.

The words you put out into the world are also important. What do you want to say? Are there times when you want to be quiet? This was something that took some learning and unlearning from me.

When I started to find my voice, I wanted to use it as much as possible. Even when the topics were something I was uninterested in or disliked, I felt like I had to be heard. There was a swing from feeling like a dismissed and quiet child to wanting to be bold. Bold is excellent, but not just for the sake of being bold.

I can write an entire book on loving yourself and knowing your worth (which is why it is showing up as such a common theme in this book). I have learned that for myself, when the conversation turns political or controversial, I would rather sit and breathe quietly because it is not something I choose to debate or take part in. Sitting there in the conversations and controlling my breath to stay balanced is now the way I contribute to conversations where I have nothing to add with my words. It is ok that people want to have those conversations, good even. That is a part of their journey; it does not mean it has to be a part of mine. I get to choose the words I use and also when I use my words, and so do you.

Find what is important to you and be loud if you choose to. It is your choice. Just because you have learned how powerful words are doesn't mean you must always use them. It is ok to be quiet too. Choosing when to use words has a power of its own. Speaking when you have something to say, instead of inserting your opinion into every topic discussed, is a beautiful skill to learn.

Be protective of your words. If you know you are in a situation where you will feel dismissed or unseen or your comments will not be received well, it is advisable to protect yourself. Ask yourself how these words will be received. Is it worth it? Would speaking up or staying quiet best save your energy? Do what feels right to you.

And the beautiful thing is, what feels right to you one day doesn't have to be what feels right the next day. You get to grow every single day. You get to choose what you do in each moment. You are constantly learning new lessons, and seeing new things, so one thing you used to have no opinion on may come into the foreground enough for you to form an opinion.

Just because you didn't speak on it last week doesn't mean you can't speak up now. You get to take a breath and decide right where you are. Do I want to use my words, or do I want to listen and use my breath? Ask yourself, is this a conversation I want to have? When we live in the now, we listen to ourselves and follow what our inner self is telling us.

Remember how powerful your words can be when you choose to speak. You are making art with what you say. I am a creative person, and so I say this. Paint pictures with your words and tell stories with them. Do with them what feels authentic to you. Have something important to say? Say it. Scream it from the rooftops, even. And know that you are brave and brilliant for speaking your truth.

This doesn't only go for you. Other people get to use their words too, and they get to do it in a way that feels authentic to them. That is not for you or me to say what their truth is. Your journey is yours; my journey is mine, and their journey is theirs.

This book is my truth in my own words. That doesn't mean you must live and breathe every word I say. I have learned what works for me, which became essential for me to share, so I am doing that. These are my essential words, and I believe wholeheartedly that everyone has their own.

Find your truth and the words inside of you that support that truth. Please share what you want to share and share it with those who will receive it. Choose the words that mean something to you and be content with that personal meaning. Let go of any expectation that anyone will understand your words; they don't have to. We can appreciate other journeys or other peoples' words. We must only love them, and when we realize that love is all we are, we can send it to anyone.

Words are either wands of light magic or weapons of dark magic. You can use them to connect to yourself and outward, or you can use them to fight against yourself and others. You can use them to stay stuck in the past or keep yourself wrapped up in thoughts of the future, or you can release yourself from those times that don't exist, and you can enjoy your presence in the present.

The choice is yours. What words will you choose?

Chapter 9:
Recreate

Re-creation
Focus on the word create
Remember to love
There is no room for hate

Hate can not
be the driver of change
Love is the winner
of that game

When you want to do something
to make you succeed
Focus on what it really
is that you need

Success comes from learning
who you want to be;
Then looking in the moments
and doing what you see.

How can you spend each moment
in a way to promote your goals?
Listen inside.
You already know

You were born with wings
You can already fly
All you have to do,
is take off toward the sky

What did you like to do when you were a child? That is an excellent place to start. You can return to that person in a lot of ways. Of course, there will be some differences, and think of the last time you could consistently stay in the moment you are in. Were you a child? You have that in common with many people, myself included.

My coach Matt has been instrumental in my re-creation of myself. When I decided to enroll in coaching with him, I thought I was only looking for support and community in my new alcohol-free lifestyle, and he has helped me with so much more. I have been able to reconnect to my inner child, heal my inner teenager, and heal and keep many relationships that could have suffered way more without the support. Matt and his Recovery Roadmap program very much supported my re-creation and redefinition.

I started with my inner child connection, looking back into what used to set my soul on fire and reconnecting to and making habits of integrating those things into my adult life.

I used to name the animals in my yard; Fred, the frog, was an all-time favorite, and guess what I do now?

You guessed it.

I still name the animals in our yard. I have told stories of this at work and have been called Snow White a few times. Harley, the heron, comes in the spring, along with Milo & Minka, the muskrats. Simon, the squirrel, is nesting in the tree outside my office window. Timmy, the turtle, shows up anytime the lake isn't frozen. I love them all; they bring me a smile and peace when I see them.

What is it that you like to do? Think back. Did you play a sport that you adored? Did you love to draw? Were you a singer? Did you want to be a chef, and did the idea of cooking beautiful dishes excite you?

Singing was one of mine, as I talked about. Writing was another, which I returned to. Writing this book is something that I can feel in my body, mind, and soul. There are times when I don't even know what I am writing. I describe it as like a trance, I am so in the zone, and then somehow, I have written thousands of words and must re-read them to ensure they are not a jumbled mess. Usually, those times are when I write my favorite work.

What lit your soul on fire when you were little? Does it still give you that feeling when you think back to it? Do you have the opportunity to incorporate that back into your life? You will find that time if you start focusing on the journey and the moments.

I didn't think I did when I was stuck in my patterns and destination-based living. My achiever pattern told me that those things were a waste of time. They didn't get me closer to any of the goals I had set for myself, so how would they help me? My people-pleaser pattern told me my hobbies didn't make anyone happy and that focusing on my wants and needs was a waste of time. Now I know that my goals are great, and I am achieving more than I ever have, but what I accomplish differs from the purpose. The purpose is the moment. I could feel the moments so much easier when I started doing the things that lit me up.

During coaching, when I started to connect more to my inner child, I remembered how much I loved singing and how comments from others when I was a little girl caused me to lose belief in myself and stop. Creativity, in general, was something I thought I had lost that I returned to and found within myself.

You are creative. We were created to create. Write songs, color pictures and books, cook food art, and develop ourselves. And because we were born to create, we can recreate.

Take me, for example. I would have told you I was not creative a year ago. I would still have told you I was a social butterfly, so more than one thing has changed for me recently.

Now, I am writing this book and writing and creating songs. I lock myself in a closet with coloring books or sketch pads. I am incredibly creative, and I always have been. I turned away from it for a while. When I started living authentically, tapping back into that side of me was effortless.

When you notice the moments, the moments slow down. When you slow down, you give yourself time to reconnect to yourself. When you are connected to yourself, you can be more productive. Slowing down will prompt speeding up.

When life feels like it is too much, too overwhelming, and too fast-moving, that is a crucial indicator that you are out of the now and either in the past or in the future.

Stop.

Take a breath, use your words, and reconnect to this moment.

An excellent way to recreate who you are is to start by writing. I am biased about being a writer, and I can still promise you that writing it out is magical. Is there something you want? Write about it. Is there some way you want to be? Write about it. A goal written down is 1,000 times more likely to happen. Some people call it journaling; some call it manifestation; others call it goal setting. Call it what you want it. If you do it, you will see direct results.

Now is where you can tell me "I thought I was supposed to stay in the moment." Why are you telling me to write about the future? Why do I even need to write about the future?

Writing about the future helps us to stop overthinking it, so at this moment, if you write out what you want, you can have a plan. The plan can go into effect immediately. Now you can start living for the moment instead of always having to wonder and overthink the future.

The same is true with writing about the past. We want to stay present and not live in the past. However, we may have stories that keep us stuck in the past. Write them out. That is the number one way to unstick stories. Writing them out equals getting them out from where they are stuck and swirling. Write them conversationally. A story in your head stays stuck, spins around, and blocks you from moving forward.

Once you write out your goals and the stories blocking you, you have cleared the space for you that you want to create. So where do we go from there? How do we start to recreate ourselves?

On the following two pages, I have left space to write your goals and fears about the future and a space to write out what chains you to the past. Write them. Read them out loud and then breathe. Write what you

feel. You are creating awareness, and awareness is key.

Write here:

Now you can start taking steps to get you there. Your plan, identify what you can do to get yourself there. If it involves talking to other people, make the phone calls immediately. Act. The more effort you take immediately, the easier it will become to continue reaching your goals. Live your life as a person who has already reached their goals.

Another mention of my coach, Mark, to reference for one of his quotes that has continued to stick with me through the years,

"Action dispels overwhelm."

Want a task to feel less overwhelmed? Start taking steps to complete the task. Then keep going, and the overwhelming feeling dissolves.

*Tip- Write your goals as "I will" statements on a separate piece of paper. You can also write them out as "I did" statements. Putting them in the past tense is a fantastic way to make your brain believe you already did what you set out to do, which also increases the likelihood of reaching that goal.

So, let's stick with the gym example.

On the sheet of paper, write, "I will go to the gym four times a week for the next six months" or "I did go to the gym four times a week for the last six months."

Go ahead and write yours out now.

Now, hang that one on your mirror next to your affirmations. Say all those statements in your mirror to yourself daily when you wake up and before you go to sleep and remember...add a big deep breath between each one.

What immediate action can you take to help you live as the person to reach your goals? Well, in this example...do you have a gym membership? If you still need to join a gym, and you know what gym you want to go to, make a call and buy your membership. If you need to know what kind of gym you want to go to, it is time to research and make some calls. Get information and find a gym. Then sign up.

Next, grab your calendar or planner. I prefer pen to paper. You can use a digital calendar if you desire. Schedule your workouts. Include the time you will go.

There you go. Your plan is solid. You now have created the identity of a person who goes to the gym four days a week. It will be much easier to integrate that goal into your life because you have put the focus on being that person.

This same method can work with most if not all, goals.

Meal prep? Research recipes, make your list, and shop for ingredients. Schedule weekly time on your calendar to do everything, then schedule the time to make the food. Write, "I did meal prep every week this year," and hang it on your mirror....and remember you get to meal prep because it will save you time during the week and help you stay nourished and satisfied.

Your goal could be to find a new job. Schedule time to job search, schedule time to apply, schedule time to interview. Write it on the mirror and get specific. "I accepted a new position in finance making $XXX,XXX in January." Remember, you get to find a new job because the perfect opportunity is out there, and you are qualified.

Once you have these goals scheduled, remember that they are not your purpose. You are whole right now. You are complete, and you are entirely worth it. It is ok and beautiful to set goals that honor yourself. Be careful not to make them your life or base your love for yourself on them. Once you set the goal, continue to live in joy and love. The consistency to reach your goals becomes much easier and you will realize and see that while you are still proud when you hit your goals, you were happy in all the moments. That is where the true beauty lies. The person you have created is a byproduct of living authentically. The attachment to the goal and the destination dissolves.

Re-creation is a fun part of healing because you can be whoever you want. Let go of your expectations, and remember that you are considering who you are, to pay attention to the authentic you. Pay attention to the patterns that you have discovered. Notice the conditioning. It is essential to be aware of that when setting goals.

There is a balance to re-creation. At the beginning of my healing journey, I was nowhere close to the moment I was in. I was completely removed from it. I was obsessed with my past stories and how I had gotten to the point of being so sad. So, I started trying to figure those out. Then once I got there, I became obsessed with the future and destination based. I only focused on who I could become if I worked harder at healing. I didn't focus on my recovery. I wasn't listening to my body or my soul. I was living fully as my pattern and ego - going after what I thought I wanted. Weight loss is a big one, to which I attached all my worth to.

"If I can reach my goal weight, I will be so happy. That is the only thing still holding me back." I thought. The translation was that I was the only one holding me back.

I had a lot to learn. The big thing is that happiness comes first, and accomplishing goals is a byproduct of joy. I was still restricting and forcing myself to the point of exhaustion. I was consistent for a while, but it was still unsustainable, severely lacking balance in my life and myself. I had an illusion of happiness at times and an illusion of sadness. I still lived in a very binary way of good vs. evil, good food vs. bad food, good meditation vs. bad meditation, good workouts vs. bad workouts, and more.

Good and bad are titles we assign, and grouping activities as good or bad causes us to miss out on all the intricacies of the moment.

I was making strides, though—steps towards learning. Re-creation does not have to be linear. And you can recreate yourself as many times as you feel necessary. You can wake up in the morning after believing you are fully healed (which I am not sure is a thing), and then 15 minutes later, you can have an awakening that shifts everything.

That is ok. We are consistently learning and growing and expanding. Recreating ourselves is a process.

I learned that all food serves its purpose. I learned to listen to my body and pay attention to the way I felt.

When I want to move, I move. When I want to sit still, I sit still. When I want to laugh, I laugh. When I want to cry, I cry. I stopped forcing myself to live as I thought I should and started living as I did.

The goal-setting process I explained earlier was also taught to in my Enlifted certification. It is beautiful process, a great way to feel organized, and you can set goals for yourself. Living with intention is gorgeous, and it is essential to remember that our worth is innate from birth. The point is to feel the moment; the destination is a distraction. Feel the moment, live in the moment, and you will be precisely where you are supposed to be.

To recreate, first, remember this. You are creative. We are born creative. It is already inside of us. You already know how to create and, in turn, how to recreate. Start listening to your creative side. I started with coloring books and colored pencils, and as I brought color to the pages, I was teaching myself how to recolor my life.

Tapping into your creative side is also a beautiful way to own the moment that you are in. As you sit down to the color, write, draw, or sing, or go outside to take pictures in nature. Whatever it is, you connect yourself to your task in real-time.

In writing a song, you focus on the music and the lyrics. You get in "the zone," and suddenly, the song is everything on your mind.

Drawing or coloring. You focus on what you are doing at the time you are doing it. You pick your colors and carefully use them for each part of the masterpiece you are creating.

Nature photography. You slow down, listen, look, and feel where you are. You focus on what is there and the shots you can take.

Creating yourself can be approached the same way. Stop. Look into yourself. Feel where you are and who you are. Feel who you want to be. What can you do at that exact moment? Think of it as art because you are art, and you are your greatest masterpiece. Believe that.

Take your time creating it, choose the colors, lyrics, and photos you want to make of yourself and realize that you can change your mind. You are allowed to redirect, and you are allowed to make perceived mistakes. You are learning and growing as you create yourself the greatest masterpiece you will ever create.

Re-creation can take however much time as you want or as is necessary. Five minutes or five years, any progress is progress, and that is what is so beautiful about expanding and growing. You can take your time. You get to decide slowly or seemingly all at once, and if you are truly listening to yourself, you will know what pace to go.

Anytime I consciously decided to listen to what I had to say and then follow what I had heard myself say, I was recreating myself. I was growing and expanding and becoming more and more my true and pure self.

And sometimes, I take breaks from healing, constantly doing, and trying to get to the next step in my creation of myself, my authentic self, and I let myself be. Remember that we are called human beings, not human doings, or healings, and allowing ourselves to be is so important.

Allow yourself days when you feel off or like you are in a funk. Those days are there to help, guide, and teach you. Off days help you grow as much, if not more, as the days you feel lighter or more.

This chapter discusses many actions you can take to get closer to where you want to be. It is important to take actionable steps. What is more important is hearing yourself and taking actionable, authentic steps.

Chapter 10:
Redefine

Butterfly,
Why do you hide your wings, dim your light?
Why do you stay down when you were born to take flight?

Why do you stay with the caterpillars still on the ground?
When you have your wings, to the earth you are not bound?

but the caterpillars, you say...they haven't transformed
and I will be alone if I do not conform.

Does loneliness hurt more than choosing not to fly?
When you know that the magic is all in the sky?

Spread your wings butterfly, fly up above
Show 'em your colors. Show 'em your love.

Fly above the others, some will ignore, some will admire
for the ones who are ready, you will inspire

Know that the flying, is really for you
because up in that sky, you learn what is true

Who are you now that you have transformed into a new person? Does it scare you that you may lose some people you used to connect with? Are you finding it difficult to be around certain loved ones? This is very common when you start to heal and become aware, especially around people you spent a lot of time with when you were living as your patterns.

Redefining relationships can be a touchy subject for some. When people see you as your pattern or as the story you created before, there may be some confusion or even resistance on their end when you start to change. Remember that you can recreate yourself as often as you want. You get to choose what you do and who you will be.

We are already connected as humans, born with a connection with everyone. We are one. This was something paramount for me to learn. Attachment is not love, and in fact, love is the opposite. Love is freeing, and love allows the journey of others.

We learn from a young age that the fairytale ending is when we find our "one true love" and our "person". I challenge this thinking to say we are our one true love and our person. We are the only people we spend our whole life with, so knowing and trusting ourselves must come first. Then we can redefine our relationships entirely.

This is not to say that we can't have beautiful relationships with other humans; we absolutely can. Find what is your authentic self, create that person, live as that person, and then find the people that align. Let your light shine on them, and their light shine on you.

Yeah, Kaitlynn, that is cool for the people aligned with me and those who think similarly, what about those who fight against my change, who tell me I am wrong for changing?

Shine on them, love them anyways, and remember you are allowed to decide what is best for you.

When we choose to change, many relationships do too. How you navigate that is up to you. I redefined most relationships I had in my life, especially after I decided to stop drinking. Yours may not come from choosing to quit drinking, and something that I have learned in my life is that when I am the one to make changes, I can expect to be the one to redefine the relationships. People will not change to meet you or start their healing journey to relate to you. The redefinition is yours to act on.

I spent a lot of time redefining the relationships in my life and falling out of the moment I was in. I would look to the future and wonder what I was supposed to do. I would think about events that were months out and get anxious thinking about it, only to have the event come and pass with little to no stress at all. I would plan out conversations in my head that never happened. I would set expectations that were unnecessary.

The future casting was often more complex than the moment and became moments I lost because I was not entirely in them.

When it came time to redefine my relationships, I had a lot of trial and error. Some friends and family were so supportive, and others tried and didn't know how to support me in a productive way.

Then others were openly not supportive of my healing journey or how I was healing.

"I didn't need that as a kid, look at me." type statements. Or "You just have to focus on the good."

Then there were the "we miss drinking with you" statements when it was clear how much happier I was without alcohol or the cringy alcohol jokes I started to become hyper-aware of.

It took me a while to realize that when defining my relationships, I first had to learn it was not about anyone else. This was my life, changing, healing, and growing. If I wanted relationships redefined, it was up to me to do it.

Changing relationships with my loved one has been an ongoing process until recently, and I am sure I will vary my approach as I continue to learn more. The method also can be different for every person. Do what feels authentic to you in each moment. Listen to yourself and trust what you need. I was still in a "figure it out" stage as in the beginning. I became more and more in the Now, my relationships started to take shape.

Some people will be very receptive to your change, see how much you are growing, and be supportive. This will mostly be people who are comfortable with themselves and their journey. The people who are resisting your growth are projecting the resistance within themselves. Remember that you get to choose what you do, and it is important to listen inside yourselves.

The most crucial point I can make when defining your relationships is that your journey is yours, and everyone else's journey is theirs. This is so important to keep in mind when communicating. It will put you in a place of loving the other person instead of trying to understand them, or worse, make them understand you.

Go into the redefinition period with love being the leader. Being love forward always wins. Always is a word I am careful with now, and here it is. Remember that we are starting with our love for ourselves, which is the source of all our love.

Remember, too, that love cannot be altered. There is no less love or no more love you can give. Love is infinite and eternal. I have family members I no longer talk to, yet I love them as much as I ever did. Love does not require understanding or conversations.

I used to struggle with the idea of removing friends and family members from my life, primarily because of my people-pleasing past. My wanting to keep everyone happy had me holding onto toxic relationships for both parties involved. The decision to remove people is for my protection and theirs too. I would no longer be a constructive or helpful part of their journey. If someone hinders your expansion or, worse, causes you to shrink back into your patterns, that is when you know that redefinition is necessary.

Most of the time, it will not come down to ending relationships. If you are holding yourself and protecting yourself, most people will support that. Even if not initially, as they see you encapsulate love and joy, they will know you are on the right path. Your passion and happiness will start to expand to them effortlessly. Not only will they see your path and that you are happy, but most people will also at least accept it. The ones who are ready will be inspired. Your inner light's glow will show them all the power that they carry within them. You will no longer have to pour from an empty cup because you are no longer giving away what is in your cup. You are overflowing and inspiring others to keep their cup full.

Love is what fills the cup that we have. That's why our cup is so quickly emptied when we depend on other people's love. Once we realize our infinite love, our cup can never become empty because we will always have the passion for filling it back up. That realization makes redefining your relationships real, lasting, and permanent.

If you are like me and have spent years giving your love light away, and people have grown used to that, you can change that for yourself. What is so beautiful is that you can do that with love. Instead of saying, "this is my love light, and you can't have it," you can say, "this is my love light, and this is how I grew it, and everyone can grow their own. This is how", and you can show them. Your love light will spread onto others without letting them have yours.

The only time it may be necessary for others to be removed from your life is when they refuse to fill their cup when they want to steal your light. You will become protective of your light, which is good. Especially if you are like me, and if you did allow your light to be stolen or diminished, or if you gave it away. When people are jealous of your light instead of happy for you for finding it, that is when caution is needed. The light is love, and love is light; anybody can light their light. Just as you and I were born with it, they only must believe it for themselves.

Some people are so stuck in their darkness that they will work to pull others into it because the darkness is lonely. Yet, it can be addicting to some, so as they sit in the darkness, they may try to drag you in with them without realizing all they have to do is walk into the light. They may try to make you put your light out to fit in with them. Nobody can take that away as long as you remember that your love light is infinite and sourced by you.

Trust yourself - you know you best. Since you have gotten this far in this book, you have done some serious thinking and inner work to get here. You already know what to do.

Remember from the chapter on words...

What is your truth? What do you have an opinion on? Where do you want to contribute, and where do you want to sit quietly, control your breath, and let other people have the conversation? Both are ok, and both are authentic to you.

How to have the conversation, and how to shift productively. The talks can be tricky to navigate. My aim for this chapter is to help you route yourself and your conversations in a way that avoids the perceived "wrong turns" I made in my journey early on.

As I explained earlier, I had issues with this in the beginning. I came in angrily at what I thought was wasted time, the time I spent in my patterns instead of as me. Realize that those times were all necessary to help you know who the pure you is. You are this version of yourself with all of the experiences you had before. Go in bold, not spiteful like I did. And realize that everything is not rigid. I let my patterns lead at the start. This is what that looked like.

"I found my voice. I need to talk about everything. I always must have an opinion. Be bold and be loud. That is who you are". That is the way I thought, anyway.

I had considered myself free, and yet I was trying to debate on political or religious topics, which held no weight to me. These topics that I didn't care about or didn't have a strong opinion on or believe that everyone is entitled to their opinion on, and here I was arguing. Becoming inauthentic from what I truly wanted to be.

Authenticity, making decisions in the moment, means just that. Being authentic did not mean I always needed to be talking just because I had found my voice. Being authentic told me I wanted to use my voice when the topic mattered to me, and I had something to say.

When you are living authentically you will also recognize how much you say by saying nothing at all, and how much control of your breath can control the situation without words.

The pendulum swings. From quiet and timid to inserting myself in every conversation and having opinions about everything. It didn't take me long to realize that it didn't feel authentic. I came up with my definition of authenticity.

Again, authenticity is listening to yourself each the moment you are in.

If there is a conversation going on and it is something you are aligned with and passionate about, contribute, be loud, and shout it from the rooftops.

Suppose there is a conversation going on that you are uncomfortable with or that you are not aligned with. Sit and breathe slowly if you want to stay. Trust me, sitting with a regulated nervous system contributes way more than you know. Also, if it is a situation where you don't want to be involved at all, let me be the first to tell you. *You are allowed to leave.*

I take full responsibility for my missteps at the beginning of the redefinition of my relationships. With my family, with my friends. I wasn't trusting myself. I often turned my insecurities into projections for others. Once I realized what I needed and started trusting, I could communicate that these were "me things." I am allowed to have triggers, and I am allowed to have situations I don't want to be in, activities I don't want to be in, and conversations I don't want to be a part of. That is not anyone else's responsibility; it is mine.

Taking accountability for myself has been paramount as well. Once you realize that your life is your responsibility and nobody else's, you can stop asking for permission to live how you want. Equally as important is to recognize that when you start living as yourself, you are not responsible for changing anyone else's journey. You can share your story; if others relate and want help, you can help them. Share the gifts and the power and drop any expectation that anyone should change because you did. You are making your choices, and they get to make theirs. And when you are living in a state of love and joy, you will only have a passion for others' journeys.

Drop the need for understanding. You do not need to understand everyone's journey. A big mistake I made was trying to be seen and understood. That is not the point.

The point is to be love and be loved. Love does not require understanding. That would be a condition.

You have the power to redefine any relationship you want, and you can do it in the way you want to. Is there a group of people you want to spend more 1-on-1 time with? Are there people you know you appreciate, and that you also like alone time after seeing them in order to recharge?

Are you like me, a highly sensitive person that was forcing myself to become a social butterfly? The socialite in me was the pattern of the girl obsessed with being liked. My truth is that what makes me feel powerful is sitting in my meditation room, which is in a closet, and reading and writing books.

A recent realization is that the people I interact with feel the same as my solitude does. While explaining this is complex, you will find the people that feel aligned.

Are you a socialite? Are you an introvert? Are you both depending on the day? Are you highly sensitive and easily overstimulated? All of that is allowed. Sometimes you want to be around people; sometimes, you want to be alone. That is authentic too. The key to redefining here is to listen to what you want. Reminder, this is my definition of authenticity. Honor yourself and honor your yeses and nos.

Boundaries

Are you saying yes to you?

Are you saying yes to yourself even when it means saying no to someone else?

Boundaries are necessary when redefining your relationships. Boundaries were something I struggled with placing at the beginning of my healing. I was over-excited, ready to put boundaries on everyone and everything. This is going to be me now. Take it or leave it. I didn't have respect or vision for the way anyone else saw the world. My boundaries became very conditional.

A big one for me was that I didn't want to be around alcohol at the beginning of my journey. I had a lot of anger and a deeply rooted hatred for alcohol. When I started realizing how different of a person booze made me, I thought there was no way anyone else could be their authentic self with alcohol in their system. I couldn't fathom that.

I started trying to control other people's lives. If I could stop drinking, they could too. There were people incredibly close to me (and to be transparent, there still are) that I felt and feel alcohol is not suitable for. It steals their authenticity and turns them into different people, as it did for me. The thing is, I know that no matter what anyone else would have said to me, I had to come to my conclusions. I had to make my decisions for myself. These people are on their journeys, and I am unsure I can help alter their paths. It is only my job to walk on my own.

It is ok that I didn't want to be around alcohol, and it is ok that drunk people annoyed me. What is not ok is that I took the things that have everything to do with me and my changes and became judgmental of others in my life. They are living their own lives. The same way I am living mine.

Healthy boundaries protect you without attacking anyone else. That is important to remember. I will allow myself 2 hours of alone time a day to recharge my battery, which is a healthy boundary. Make your life about you and let everyone else live their way and remember you don't have to understand them. You don't even have to agree with them, and you can still love them because love does not have conditions.

It is easy to want to push certain things away or not let them come to the surface. You may realize feelings you were suppressing when you start to heal, which can make redefining difficult as well. Keeping in mind that everything that happened in your life was a part of your path, and got you to this moment, reading this book and looking into and listening to yourself, is an excellent reminder that every past version of you was necessary.

You are right where you are supposed to be, and so is the other person you are redefining the relationship with. Knowing that you are on two journeys, you don't need to understand and keep the conversation moving forward. Go into those conversations, remember you are loved, and allow what comes to come.

To wrap up this chapter, here is a visualization that came to me in a breathwork session that was a life-changing vision for me.

The River

A river flowing.

It appears to be calm.

You can't see the boxes chained to the bottom holding "monsters" thrashing. The boxes contain words like manipulation, betrayal, anger, fear, and sadness.

The River keeps flowing. With the boxes chained to the bottom, the River thinks she's ok as long as nobody can see the chains rip her apart from her depths. She flows steadily on the surface. As long as nobody can tell, she will be ok.

As the River starts to heal her relationship with herself, the chains begin to dissolve, and the River realizes that these chains were made up of her own doing. The toxic substance she allowed into herself, her negative self-image, and the need to be loved and adored by everyone who saw her.

As she heals more and more, all the chains disappear, and the boxes with the monsters float to the surface.

Even though the River is nervous that her monsters are now on display, the original feeling is a relief because she can finally relax without the pain of the chains ripping away at her foundation.

The boxes flow on the surface for a while, with the monsters still trapped inside. The River is free, and while the boxes are on the surface, the monsters are still contained inside, flowing on the surface.

Until the monsters, all meet at the same spot in the River, they create a dam while still thrashing inside. The boxes crash against each other. The river clogs and stops at the dam. The River knows she must allow the clog. Allow the monsters to thrash; she knows the boxes will eventually break from crashing into one another.

The River fears what will happen when the boxes open, what will happen once the monsters swim free.

Eventually, the boxes break, and what falls out are not monsters. What they are is big, beautiful, bright, and vibrant fish. Fish that belonged in the River the whole time.

Once the boxes break, the River can flow freely. The fish can swim as part of the River.

The self-imposed boxes and chains caused the River her pain all along. All the fish wanted was to be seen, to be loved, and to be free.

The River is me.

Chapter 11:
Allow

It's ok to feel
what you're feeling
If you're calm and still
Or if you're reeling

It is ok if you are excited
or feeling happy
It is ok if there is anger
or if you're sad and sappy

What is important to remember
and to know
Every feel you're feeling
is there to help you grow

Allow, Allow, Allow.

The word allow is a game changer. Stopping the fight is the definition of allowing. Whatever emotion, whatever situation you are in, you can be ok with if you think to yourself the word "allow". When you know that you can sit with any emotion and learn that you will be ok and grow through that emotion, magic happens.

Let go of the idea of good days and bad days. Assigning these labels to your day causes you to miss the moments. When you chunk an entire day into either good or bad, you do not see the moments, the emotion, and the thoughts as objective. You judge why they are there; you give them a generalized feeling instead of allowing them to be there and living in each moment.

When you learn that all emotions are neutral, you can avoid the roller coaster feeling that can occur daily. Feel what is happening and truly take it all in. Allowing what is there enables you to feel all the joy, whether that joy is from cheer and excitement or whether that joy is from learning a new lesson and growing through heaviness and gloominess. Allowing you to be where you are without casting judgment on it and, in turn, allows you to realize everything that is happening in each moment. The beauty in life comes from allowing what is there without pushing it away with external sources or distractions.

Learning to allow is pivotal to growth. Every topic covered in this book is fantastic and helpful, and if you take one word from the entire thing, I want that word to be "allow." Allowing what comes, allowing what is out of your control, and allowing whatever is there to be there, loving what is there, knowing that it serves its purpose.

Many professionals in the self-help, coaching, or therapy space will tell you to create, take action, and control your thoughts and emotions. To grab life by the horns, to steer your ship. While there is a time and place for intentional creation (such as everything discussed in the re-creation chapter), it is important to allow the twists and turns of life's paths. Life will not always be in your control. Your emotions may catch you off guard. You may see something that prompts an unexpected response. That is ok. That is beautiful. Remember? The only bad feeling is an emotion that is halted before it is felt all they way through. So, when this heavy emotion comes up, remember that it is supposed to be there. This is where allowing comes in.

I have used loving as the opposition to fighting our emotions. Allowing is another significant opposition. We can teach ourselves or be taught that allowing emotions is weak. Allowing emotional responses is inappropriate or, worse, damaging to ourselves. Allowing and love go hand in hand. If you allow an emotion to be there, you love it and see it. If you love all feelings, you will enable them to be there.

How many of you have had these two words said to you before?

"Don't cry."

or

"Stop crying"

As an HSP, I take the opposite approach to this.

Cry. Lose control. Let it go. Let the tears flow. Let the pain be painful. As the tears flow out of your body, so do the emotions. So does the pain. We learn to trap our tears, and in that, we learn to trap our pain. Push it down into our body. Where it stays, it lives.

When people say, "Cry it out," that is good advice; much better advice than "Don't cry." You are crying the feelings out; you are feeling them all the way through. Crying is energy. As you release the tears from the body, the energy flows with it. So, while it may be painful, it is also beautiful.

Remember this…

All emotions feel good. The hierarchy of emotions being positive and negative is an egoic human concept. Emotions are neutral.

Painful emotions and beauty exist simultaneously...if you allow them to.

We can learn to hide emotions in many different situations. Such as being made fun of in school for crying, or parents who dismissed emotions and told you to stop throwing a fit or control yourself, instead of sitting with you to understand and discuss what caused the emotion to be there.

As I write these words, I am practicing them myself. Allowing grief. Allowing trauma responses. Allowing everything I am feeling and knowing that it all holds beauty.

Breathwork and meditation have been instrumental in allowing me to allow everything that comes. I sit down to breathe or meditate and immediately start listening. It may not feel immediate initially but keep practicing; it will get easier and more accessible. When I listen and hear so clearly, I can see more clearly, too. I see how much power every part of my life can hold.

It is vital to bring this up because I know people will ask, "so I am allowed just to have a temper tantrum in adulthood?"

Well, yes, and you also have been taught how to be productive in feeling, and the need for a full-on tantrum will dissolve as you feel emotions as they come up.

Learning to feel and allow will decrease the need for a temper tantrum, and as an adult, you will be so much better equipped to love the feeling once you learn to allow it all the way through. See, the more you feel, the more the emotion and intensity of those feelings won't feel so strong.

Tantrums come from compounded, unfelt emotions.

When you learn to push down and stop crying before you are done, you leave that emotion in your body. Over time that residual feeling builds up in your body.

Have you ever argued about something small and made a huge deal? Afterward, wondering where it came from, apologizing to the other person because you overreacted. Think about it, where do those overreactions, that boiling over feeling, come from? Often those come from that pushing down of emotions.

We are supposed to feel. That is how we keep ourselves calm, where our nervous system is regulated. Allow what is there to be there.

Allowing is a practice, and it certainly takes practice to learn. I have been repeating the affirmation: *"I am allowing"* in my bathroom mirror for months. Allowing is important to me, one of the most important skills I learned, so I will continue to practice it.

Allowing comes into play, more than only, in the emotions that you are feeling. So many of life's circumstances are out of our control, and when you learn that everyone is on their journey, you realize even more how much is out of your control. And when you learn to allow it, you learn to release your responsibility from things you can't control. So many people are walking around, carrying experiences and emotions that are not theirs. They don't belong to them. It is time to put down others' feelings to be fully in touch with their own.

So, start now; let go of other people's journeys. Allow them to live their life the way that they see fit. They are here to learn their lessons; you are here to discover yours.

When we learn to allow and start to master it, we free ourselves from other people's guilt and shame. We can support others and love them without attaching their journeys to ours.

Focus on what you can control and allow the rest. Love it all. Allow the emotions to be there and let go of the need to save everyone or keep everything together.

Allow what is there to be there and keep yourself together.

Visualization

Imagine a pot of water - no flame, no boil, calm.

Small flame underneath that is fielded by emotions that have yet to be resolved. As we start to feel, the flame turns up. The water begins to heat up. We push the feeling down while the flame stays where we left it. We carry that feeling with us, and the water inside starts to heat up more, not enough to make the water boil yet.

We continue on our way, feeling only comfortable feelings. Then we run into another uncomfortable feeling. We don't want to feel that one, so we push that down inside. The flame underneath turns up higher. The water starts to agitate and begins to warm up more. Not quite at a boil, but you can see the movement in the water; you feel the pot start to get hot. Then another uncomfortable feeling comes along, and you push that one down too. The flame is fully on. The water is now boiling over. The pot could not contain the burning flame underneath. Realizing now, the only way to stop the boil is to turn off the flame, and we go back. We feel each emotion that we push away one by one. The flame returns slowly to a simmer, and the water relaxes. We learn to keep the pot at a comfortable temperature; we feel our feelings as we go. We heal before the emotions build up. There are never enough unresolved emotions to light the flame. The water never boils.

Chapter 12:

Expand

In my belief, I am here on this Earth
Not to prove, to recognize my worth

I thought it was something to achieve
Now I know it has always been in me

Life was for getting somewhere externally
Now life is inside and I am learning to be

Be in this moment. Stay in the Now
Stop questioning why and stop wondering how

Trust myself. I already know
To my past and my future it is time to let go

Let go and be who I was meant to
I already know in me what is true

Hold on to myself, take my own hand
Jump all in, time to expand

We're here to learn, grow, and expand.

Are you expanding or shrinking to fit in because it feels safe in the middle? We have a herd mentality. In the middle of the herd, we are safe. We are guarded. We blend in.

Being this far into this book, let me make something clear to you—something that I already know about you.

You are not supposed to be in the middle of the herd. You are born to stand out. To lead, to help the herd know that they can make their own decisions, and while we are all connected, we also get to be whoever we want. We get so wrapped up in what is relevant to our world and what we see. Let me tell you something: you have already permitted yourself and are already expanding.

Getting wrapped up in external sources can cause us to shrink. When I used to watch the news, I thought I had to have an opinion on everything they talked about. Politics, religion, social issues. I had to know it all. That's what was going on in my world. I have learned this.

The news, reality TV, the sports. I was making them part of my identity, a part of me. They are not a part of me. You are allowed to watch and be entertained. The problem comes when we attach to using these external sources to distract.

Love and connection are expansive. Listen to the silence because, in silence, you hear yourself. That is where you learn what is truly you. Get comfortable sitting with yourself. Fall in love with sitting alone with yourself. You are the one person you spend every waking minute with. Do you want it to be a partnership and a friendship, or do you want to be in a war against yourself? Listening inside yourself is the way to hear what you need to expand.

Expansion is so beautiful. Waking up to who you are and who you have always been at your core is remarkable. The pure you, you in the Now, you that lives from moment to moment. That is the most expanded version of you.

Have you been questioning parts of this book? Have you been examining aspects of your life? Are you on the correct path? Those questions are allowed; it is ok if you do not always have the answer. Trust your path. You do not need to know where it is leading. It is the right path, and you are going the right way.

All paths are correct because there is no destination to get to. If you focus on the journey, you will find joy and beauty in whatever direction you take. So, walk on your path firmly, knowing there is joy in every step you take. While at times you will have an idea of where you are heading, be open to the idea that you may hear the universe tell you to redirect. Be open to the idea that there may be bumps, stops, and detours along the way too. It is ok, keep walking. And walk not to get anywhere, but to enjoy the walk.

You can stop questioning yourself now and expand. It is really that simple. Questions will come up. And that is ok. Allow them to. Guess what? The answers to the questions are optional. Even the questions are distractions. Questioning yourself can pull you from the moment. Notice the question. If you know the answer, answer it; if you don't, see the question. Leave it alone and return to your moment.

How do you know if you are expanding? Well, let me tell you this. Again, I know you are growing because you reached for a book like this. Are you all the way developed? You have made tremendous strides, and there is no such thing as fully expanded. Expansion is an ongoing process. I am still expanding. The most expanded person in the world is still expanding. One of the best ways to grow is to know there is no limit or end to growth. There is no becoming fully expanded, which is beautiful because it means that we get to keep growing as long as we are alive. How cool is that?

Expansion is simple; however, simple is not always easy, and simple is sometimes painful. As I write these words, I am smack dab in the middle of a very painful expansion. I am crying it out. Remember that crying is allowed and supposed to be loved. Crying is supposed to happen, and stifling my tears would stifle my feelings. Suppressing my feelings would be stifling expansion, and that would cause me to shrink. Feeling my feelings allows me to expand into love.

My patterns are all dissolving, and some are so deeply rooted that they are clinging to me, and even though I am aware of them, sometimes they come up when I am not anticipating them. When I dig deep, I still feel the little girl that wanted to keep everything together, to rid her entire world of conflict and division. All she wanted was to keep everyone smiling and cheerful, even at the expense of her happiness or acceptance. From the start, she was a little love light, but her patterns taught her to sacrifice herself to build everyone up.

And I feel her, I feel her right now, and I am allowing her to be here. I let her be seen and loved, but the pattern is no longer steering my life. The little love light is.

The world is you. The world is as you. Everyone you talk to will mirror how you see yourself somehow. Do you see yourself as growing and expanding and loving? Love is the big one. As you expand, you become closer and closer to that pure love being. And as you become more and more loved, you will attract more and more love. People will start to grow around you. Your love will lift them into their love. Not at the same rate, and some people will still stay stuck longer, and it will still happen. It is starting to happen around me, and it is impressive to see.

My expansion is for me, though, and when you expand, expand first for you; the magic is for you. What happens to other people as you expand is a beautiful byproduct of you realizing you are all that is. Every person and every experience you have ever had is you and is what your life will be. You already know you are here to expand, and you want to.

Addictions, reality TV, gossip, social media. Those are distractions that stop us from listening, and we must listen to expand. Sit with yourself for an hour. Don't reach for your phone. If that is too much of a jump, start with a walk, and don't bring your phone. Notice what you hear, what nature says to you, and what you say to yourself.

And listen to it.

For a long time, I heard myself. I heard that I was not on the path I wanted to be on. I didn't want to restrict my food to the point that I'd get dizzy, and I didn't want to drink myself into a different person. I would hear the voices, but I had become addicted to stopping them. I had become addicted to shrinking. So, I kept shrinking until the universe got louder, my inner voice got louder, and I started healing.

When you break free of those external distractions holding you back and start to look inward, that is when you grow. It goes back to this. You already know what you want. You already know what you are (love). You already know what to say, and you already know what to do. It is time to start listening to that knowledge. When you look inside and listen and then act on what you are hearing…that is an expansion and living in the moment.

What happens if we do not expand, you ask? Well, occasionally, we stay the same size, and we move through life that way. More likely, though, we shrink. Most of the time, you have two choices, expand into your pure you or shrink into the patterns and distractions. If we are living in the Now, you are likely expanding. Otherwise, you are shrinking into whatever takes you out of the now; this could be different addictions like alcohol, drugs, codependency on another, need for approval, work, destination-based living, or negative self-talk.

If you spend time where you are and honestly with yourself, you will hear what your expansion requires. You will be able to look at all parts of your life objectively, and if you choose to listen to and live the way your inner knowing is telling you to, you will expand. And it will start to become automatic.

Anything other than expansion will start to feel incredibly painful once you realize what your pure and expanded self feels like. Comfort zones will become extremely uncomfortable, and the feeling of fear will start to become more exciting. You will know then that when you are scared, it is because you are walking into a period of extraordinary and beautiful growth.

You will drop the need to feel ready before doing something and realize that "ready" is a choice, not a feeling, as you thought. You will act because it is something you want now. Fears of the future will no longer be able to stop you from going after what you genuinely wish because the idea of not reaching for it will be more painful.

If you attempt something and fail, you will know that that was a path you were supposed to be on, and all the lessons that you learned will become vividly clear. You will learn, and you will listen to yourself. If the voice tells you to keep going this way, you will. If the voice points out a new road, you will happily veer that way, knowing the road you were on led you here.

There will be no more "wastes of time." There will be no more mistakes. There will only be roads that veer or fork into another road, which are all necessary for your destination-less journey.

You can put your past down and drop the worries and thoughts of the future. You are here. Remember that many times what you fear and resist the most is what will bring you the most growth. This helps to move through the resistance, knowing it is only a sign of glorious expansion.

See, fear used to stop me dead in my tracks. "No, that is scary, so I am going to quit." Now fear is excitement. It is still scary, and now I know that on the other side of that fear, I will find out something about myself and all that is. I am on this human journey, and I will use it to grow and learn as much as I can in the time that I have.

Everything in the world is a mirror of me, and I am in love. Looking at it this way, loving myself and everything around me is much easier. It is necessary to love the lightness in you. It is also necessary to love the darkness in you. It is a part of the human version of you. Let it be there. Allow it and see it, and when someone mirrors that back to you, allow it from that person, see it, and love it. I love everything that is there.

You are only love, so you can only love. There is no such thing as good or bad. There is only love.

Visualization

Floating in an ocean, waves crashing and moving in all directions. You fight to stay afloat and must challenge these waves and take them head-on. You punch and kick at the waves as you swim, barely moving. The waves keep getting bigger - more challenging and brutal to fight. You are getting exhausted; you want to stop fighting. Your energy is depleting, and you are tired of fighting the waves.

You can stop fighting. Remembering that you can float, you stop swimming, turn over, and lay on the waves. Realizing when you stop fighting the waves, they will carry you. The waves are supposed to be there, and you are supposed to work with them. Allow the waves because the waves are you.

To focus on and practice (this is a great thing to hold in your mind when meditating or doing breathwork) is that of an ocean. The waves are your emotions and thoughts. You can swim and fight and thrash in the waves. You can use all your energy and tire yourself fighting the waves or stop fighting. You can turn over, and you can float. Remember that you can float. Allow the waves because they are going to be there, and they get to be there. They can carry when you use them for you instead of against you. You can rest on them.

Chapter 13:

Set You Free

Here we go, the choice is for you.
This is where you choose what to do

Do you continue on the way you have been going?
Or do you change your path? time for knowing

Knowing that it is time to spread your wings
And trust and believe in what that brings

Know that the moment is all that you get
And notice the beauty within it.

The time has come now, the time to let go
And the time to expand, the time to grow

So, get up on your feet and open the door
And know you are stepping into so much more

Believe in yourself, believe you are all
Till you can run, walk. Till you can walk, crawl

Start making the moves, believing in yourself
And see in your life, the moments create wealth

Time to spread your wings and fly.

You are already aware that you have wings. Getting to this point in this book proves that. If these words resonate enough with you, you are ready to fly or likely already flying. You may hesitate, though, or question if it is ok to fly, thinking, "my friends, my family, other people I know...they don't have wings yet. How do I leave them? Do I leave them?"

You don't have to leave them. The only thing you must do is realize that you are in your moment. You want you to be in your Now, not their now. You can fly around them and talk to them from the sky. Remember, they are on their journey, and you can choose yours. You will find a tribe up in the sky, and they will be magical.

Show those on the ground your beautiful wings and talk of all the magic you have found while you are in the sky. Inspire them. They have wings, too; remember, we are born with everything we need. If they are ready, they will fly with you.

Some people will be too stubborn, stuck, or addicted to the ground to see and use their wings. Some, though, will already be in the sky. Fly with them. Fly free. You will inspire some people to see their power and know they can fly. The people who are stuck or addicted will stay on the ground, and you will be able to love them from the sky. You will still be able to interact with them from there. They may not understand the sky, and the sky may scare them. They have yet to learn about all of the growth beyond fear.

It is ok if people are still on the ground; you love them the same as those in the sky. You are allowed to be with the others in the sky, though, for they are aligned with you in the same spot. They flourish in the same environment as you do. As long as the others on the ground support your flight, keep them. Be careful with those who tell you to stop flying and that your flight is dangerous or wrong. Or worse, those that try to take your wings because they refuse to see their own.

I lived my life for other people. I used to say I felt like I was born to be a pawn in everyone else's life instead of having my own. My purpose on earth was to make other people smile. That's what I wanted to do. I tried to make other people happy.

The above is true; I still have a deep compassion for making others happy and have learned that I come first. I know now my happiness was mine and other people's happiness was theirs to create. See, I wanted to help others smile, so I allowed my smile to be stolen, or at times I even willingly gave it away. Expansion for me could never have happened how I lived previously. I had to learn who I was. I had to realize that I was necessary and that it was ok to prioritize me.

Once you learn that you are yours, your expansion can start to happen at a rapid speed. And the expansion will allow you to keep yourself consistent in the moments you are in. Once you begin to expand, staying there will become effortless and natural. You will be able to see what the Now is. You will learn to stop questioning the decisions that you are making because you will see them much more clearly, without the past and future getting involved in that decision. Expand into your most pure you, and you become the most authentic you.

This book is full of everything you can do to help yourself expand. However, reading the book is just the beginning. It is important to remember that sometimes the most beautiful expansion can feel the most painful. Pain is ok. Pain is necessary, and pain is beautiful. After pain, there is growth.

You expand by knowing that we are here to feel and that the point of life is the journey. You are the moment, and you are forever. Read that again. You are the moment, and you are forever. You can stay in the Now, and if you find yourself falling out of the moment or being thrown out of it, you will become more and more aware of it.

Something that often comes up for me is feeling like I am not being my true self, my awake self, or in a situation where I feel like my light is underappreciated.

Shine anyways.

You are not shining for anyone else, expanding for anyone else, and not living for anyone else. If your shine is seen and admired or inspiring to some, that is amazing and the byproduct of living authentically as you. You are shining for you, and you are shining because you have embodied love in its purest form.

Here is what I see. The journey that I am on does not have an end destination anymore. When I started my healing journey, I thought I would eventually reach where I was "healed." The healing journey would be over, and I now had pure happiness.

That is not quite it. I do have pure happiness, and the journey continues. It is a blessing that I get to be happy right now, and I still get to continue expanding. I am focused on my healing journey and no longer the destination of healing.

I am constantly learning, growing, evolving, and expanding. There is nothing I need to heal. My past happened, and it is no longer a part of me. My future is not a part of me yet. So, what do I have? Let's say it all together now.

This moment.

Remember that to set yourself free, you must realize that this journey is yours, and you get to decide. That is how you liberate yourself from living a destination-based life, living as a pattern and getting lost in the daily grind.

You can still be kind and help others if that feels authentic. This is something I learned too. Living for yourself and setting yourself free does not mean you stop caring about others. Living for yourself means recognizing that you are here to listen to and get to know you.

You are free now. Free from whatever was chaining you to your past, free from what dragged you into the future. You can live here, in this time, in this now, because you are the Now.

Visualization

A rock chained to your back holding you back.

A rope tied to your chest pulling you forward.

The rock is the past. The rope, the future.

You move through your days, unable to feel the moment because all you can focus on is the heaviness of the rock and the pulling of the future. The rock and the rope take up all of your thoughts and all of your energy. The being between the two is ignored, and the moment you are in is dismissed.

Only when you stop and look at the being do you see the rock is on a very thin chain, and the rope is tied in a simple knot. All you have to do to free yourself is release the two, let go of the rock and let the rope fall away from you.

Now you can focus where you are. Right here. You are free.

You are Now

and Now is Love

Thank you for taking this journey with me.
Here is where I set you free.
And you get to be.

You have learned that the moment is all of all.
Take that knowledge and stop the brawl.
In love with yourself, fall.

Stay right here where you are, stay in the now.
Stop questioning why, and let go of how.
Remember to allow.

Know that each path you are on is right.
It is up to you to ignite
Your light.

Your light that has always been there down deep inside.
Anyone who said different lied.
Do not hide.

You are beauty and so is everything that is real.
Reminder to feel,

and to heal.

Now the time has come for this book to end.
For reading this, you I commend.
Thank you, my friend.

Your decision to pick up this book means the world to me. The amount of expansion I have felt in the last two years is a gift, and I am so thankful to have shared this with you. Thank you for reading how I turned my story into something beautiful by learning to trust that I am joy and love. My wish for this book is that as you put it down, my words will stay with you, and you will have learned that you carry all your power, and your story belongs to you. You get to choose. Do you want to start feeling the beauty in each moment?

I am proud of you. The fact that you not only bought this book and now read it to the end means you are already growing and ready to grow even further. You have been through a big realization or multiple realizations to get to this point, even if you didn't know when the expansion was happening. Remember that growth can sometimes feel like pain, and once you learn to sit with it, you will see in times of distress that you are prepping for change even before you know what the lesson is.

You will be awake to the patterns within you, whether you learned them to survive or were conditioned by an authority figure or our caretaker's words. You will be able to see clearly when you are not living as your most authentic version, and you will be able to dissolve the pattern as they show up. Remember, though, stop the fight and start the love. Love these patterns all the way. Know this, the patterns took care of you when you needed them to. Do not be angry at the pattern because the pattern was part of getting you to the Now. See the pattern and love it, and you will be able to live in harmony until the pattern sees that you no longer need it to be safe, and it will start to dissolve.

Remember that we are continuously learning and unlearning. You are allowed to unlearn for the rest of your life. We may have been born with some traits, some we picked up along the way, and you can unlearn anything that does not feel pure and true to you.

Nourish yourself, mind, body, and soul, and remember how much deeper nourishment goes than food. Remember that nutrition looks different to any individual. Once you learn to listen to your intuition, you will know what you need to nourish yourself fully. That could be food, nature, rest, deep breathing, or many other things.

Breathe intentionally, and remember that when you slow your breathing, the days and moments follow suit. Breath can bring you into the present very fast, focus on intentional breathing and ensure you are using your breath to energize and not exhaust you. Breath can provide you will stillness, openness, clarity, and many physical benefits, all helpful and pivotal in keeping your mind, body, and spirit where you are.

Being able to move is a gift and one we should cherish. Movement is not a punishment, and we should not be moving in a way that hurts or feels like we are depleting ourselves. You can lift heavy and run fast. You can push yourself, and make sure that you are listening to your body and moving in a way that sets your body up for feeling great. If you feel aligned in your body and are living pain-free, it can be much easier to stay out of future concerns for your health. Prioritize your health in a way that is right for you.

You can recreate yourself repeatedly. Day by day, you can see new visions, learn new sights, and have new awakenings. Allow the shifts and recreate yourself again. Remember that you are no longer creating yourself to be who anyone else wants you to be. You are creating yourself for you, for the person you want to be. For the person who supports being there moment by moment. For the person who releases the past and the future and surrenders into the Now, whatever it may bring. Look inside what sparks joy in your soul. What do you want to be doing now? What creates you want to be? Do that.

As you change, so might relationships along the way. Remember you are the one evolving which means it is your responsibility to redefine the relationships, whether that means setting boundaries or maintaining space, or on some occasions loving someone from afar, you get to choose. Remember, though, just because we are redefining our relationships doesn't mean we love anyone less. We are already connected to everything, and love is infinite. Redefine for yourself and know that any path you choose is the path you are supposed to be on.

So, allow the paths. Allow the feelings. Allow the moments to come with whatever comes up for you. Feel all the way through. Remember that any emotion you feel is good as long as you can feel it. We, as humans, have created a hierarchy of emotions. In reality, all feelings are unique and beautiful; part of the human experience is allowing and feeling them all.

Expand into all that you are. Because you are all that is, and the moment you are in is all you have. Expand into the now. Listen to yourself right here. Breathe into yourself. Sit in silence. Accept yourself. Let go of expectations and expand into pure love and joy. Allow yourself to expand through every day. Expansion can come after lightness or heaviness, and expansion is always beautiful. Learn to see that beauty and grow with it. Grow into it. Grow as it.

Release yourself and set yourself free. Set yourself free from anything other than what is in this moment with you. The past is gone; remember it, learn its lesson, and let it be gone. You are not your past, and you are the Now. The future has yet to happen. You can set goals and know some of what's coming, and you are not your future; you are the Now. Be the Now, live as the Now, and you will set yourself free to experience everything life offers. Right here, in the moment you're in.

Experience it all. Love it all.

With gratitude and infinite love,

Kaitlynn

About the Author

Kaitlynn Mika is an *Enlifted* Certified, Confidence and Clarity Coach. Her coaching career began when she embarked on her own healing journey. As she began walking that path, she learned of all the twists and turns and forks in the road. The shift for Kaitlynn was when she realized that all she had was the moment she was in, and from that day forward made it a mission to stay there. When worrying about the future or staying stuck because in the past, she realized she was missing the moments and letting the years get lost. Once Kaitlynn began her journey, it became her mission to share all the gifts she had learned with others. She is now a Level 2 Enlifted Coach and works with many different people helping them increase their confidence and get clear about what they want out of the moment. She works the stories of the past, and helps others move towards the person they want to be, while also seeing all the beauty that every moment has to offer. Kaitlynn is still very much living her journey and is thrilled to be able to share that journey with you today.

Made in United States
North Haven, CT
28 June 2023

38340090R00114